MW00979342

Crystallization-Study
of
Galatians

Volume One

The Holy Word for Morning Revival

Witness Lee

Living Stream Ministry
Anaheim, CA • www.lsm.org

© 2004 Living Stream Ministry

All rights reserved. No part of this work may be reproduced or transmitted in any form or by any means—graphic, electronic, or mechanical, including photocopying, recording, or information storage and retrieval systems—without written permission from the publisher.

First Edition, January 2004.

ISBN 0-7363-2500-X

Published by

Living Stream Ministry
2431 W. La Palma Ave., Anaheim, CA 92801 U.S.A.
P. O. Box 2121, Anaheim, CA 92814 U.S.A.

Printed in the United States of America

04 05 06 07 08 09 10 / 10 9 8 7 6 5 4 3 2 1

Contents

Preface

1. This book is intended as an aid to believers in developing a daily time of morning revival with the Lord in His word. At the same time, it provides a limited review of the Winter Training held December 22-27, 2003, in Anaheim, California, on the "Crystallization-study of Galatians." Through intimate contact with the Lord in His word, the believers can be constituted with life and truth and thereby equipped to prophesy in the meetings of the church unto the building up of the Body of Christ.

2. The entire content of this book is taken primarily from the *Crystallization-study Outlines: Galatians,* the text and footnotes of the Recovery Version of the Bible, selections from the writings of Witness Lee and Watchman Nee, and *Hymns,* all of which are published by Living Stream Ministry.

3. The book is divided into weeks. One training message is covered per week. Each week presents first the message outline, followed by six daily portions, a hymn, and then some space for writing. The message outline has been divided into days, corresponding to the six daily portions. Each daily portion covers certain points and begins with a section entitled "Morning Nourishment." This section contains selected verses and a short reading that can provide rich spiritual nourishment through intimate fellowship with the Lord. The "Morning Nourishment" is followed by a section entitled "Today's Reading," a longer portion of ministry related to the day's main points. Each day's portion concludes with a short list of references for further reading and some space for the saints to make notes concerning their spiritual inspiration, enlightenment, and enjoyment to serve as a reminder of what they have received of the Lord that day.

4. The space provided at the end of each week is for composing a short prophecy. This prophecy can be composed by considering all of our daily notes, the "harvest" of our inspirations during the week, and preparing a main point

with some sub-points to be spoken in the church meetings for the organic building up of the Body of Christ.

5. The *Crystallization-study Outlines: Galatians* were compiled by Living Stream Ministry from the writings of Witness Lee and Watchman Nee. The outlines, footnotes, and references in the Recovery Version of the Bible are by Witness Lee. All of the other references cited in this publication are from the published ministry of Witness Lee and Watchman Nee.

Winter Training

(December 22-27, 2003)

CRYSTALLIZATION-STUDY
OF GALATIANS

Banners:

God's intention is for Christ
to be wrought into His chosen people
that they may become sons of God
for His corporate expression.

We need to be rescued
out of the present evil age
by the revelation of God's Son in us.

To live the Christian life is
to live the processed Triune God
as the consummated Spirit.

God's goal is the divine sonship
for His corporate expression
as the household of the faith,
the new creation, and the Israel of God.

The Focal Point of the Divine Revelation in the Book of Galatians

Scripture Reading: Gal. 1:15-16; 2:20; 4:19; 3:26-28; 6:15

Day 1 I. **The most crucial and mysterious matter revealed in the Bible is that God's ultimate intention is to work Himself in Christ into His chosen people (Eph. 3:17a; 4:4-6):**
  A. God's desire to work Himself into our being is the focal point of the divine revelation in the Scriptures (Rom. 8:9-10, 6, 11).
  B. The book of Galatians reveals that God's intention is for Christ to be wrought into His chosen people that they may become sons of God for His corporate expression (1:15-16; 2:20; 4:19; 3:26; 6:10, 16).

Day 2 II. **The book of Galatians presents a comparison of God's two economies—His Old Testament economy and His New Testament economy (3:22-29):**
  A. The word for God's Old Testament economy is *law,* and the word for God's New Testament economy is *Christ* (v. 24).
  B. Paul experienced a genuine conversion, a real turn from God's old economy of law to His new economy of Christ (1:13-16).
  C. Christ, the Spirit, the new creation, and our spirit are the four basic things covered in this book as the underlying thought of God's New Testament economy (2:20; 3:2; 6:15, 18).

Day 3 D. God's New Testament economy is to dispense Himself as the processed and consummated Triune God into our being to be our life and our everything to make Himself one with us and us one with Him so that we may express Him in a corporate way for eternity (Rom. 8:10, 6, 11; 12:4-5; Rev. 21:2, 9-10).

E. It is not God's intention to have a group of good people; God wants many sons who are one with Him organically and who possess His life and nature and who thus can be members of the Body of Christ (Rom. 8:14; 12:4-5).

F. God's New Testament economy is the dispensing of Himself into His chosen and redeemed people to make them His sons; therefore, sonship is the focal point of God's economy (Gal. 4:4-6).

G. As we read the book of Galatians, we need to see that God's New Testament economy is to put us into Christ and to impart Himself as the all-inclusive life-giving Spirit into us to produce an organic union—an organic oneness in life—between us and the Triune God so that we may become His corporate expression (3:27-28; 4:19; 6:10, 16).

Day 4 III. **Galatians reveals that Christ is versus religion with its law (2:16, 20):**

A. Galatians deals with the law given by Moses and with the religion formed according to this law (4:21; 1:13-14).

B. The law, the base of Judaism, has been terminated and replaced by Christ (Rom. 10:4; Gal. 2:16).

C. The book of Galatians deals strongly with deviation from Christ by going back to the law (5:1-2, 4).

D. The desire of God's heart cannot be satisfied by our efforts to keep the law; His desire can be satisfied only if we remain with Christ and live Him out (Phil. 1:21a).

E. To hold to the law after Christ has come is against the basic principle of God's New Testament economy (Gal. 4:21; 5:4):

1. It is rebellion against God's economy to snatch people from Christ and to bring them back to the law.

2. Since Christ has come, the function of the law has been terminated; therefore, Christ must replace the law in our life for the fulfillment of God's eternal purpose (3:23-25).

F. The three main negative things dealt with in Galatians are the law, the flesh, and religion; these three go together, for when we are under the law, we are involved with both the flesh and religion (2:16; 3:3; 1:13-14; 6:14).

G. Paul's burden in Galatians was to reveal Christ in such a way that He would be not only the focal point of God's economy but also the focal point of our daily walk (1:15-16).

Day 5 & Day 6

IV. **God's New Testament economy is not with man in the old creation but with man in the new creation through the resurrection of Christ (6:14-15; 1:1):**

A. The main issue in Galatians is not circumcision or uncircumcision, religion or no religion; it is an issue of whether or not we are a new creation through an organic union with the Triune God (6:15).

B. Apparently Paul wrote the book of Galatians to deal with the law; actually this book deals with the old creation.

C. The new creation is altogether different from any kind of religion; religion is part of the old creation, and everything practiced in the religious world is part of the old creation (v. 14).

D. Galatians brings us to the new creation by way of the inward revelation of the living person of the Son of God (v. 15; 1:15-16).

E. The new creation is the mingling of God with man (John 15:4; 1 John 4:15):

1. The meaning of the new creation is that the processed and consummated Triune God mingles Himself with us and constitutes us with Himself to make us new (Eph. 4:4-6, 24; Col. 3:10-11).

  2. Although we remain God's creatures, we are nonetheless mingled with the Creator.
  3. Because we are now one with the Creator, His life becomes our life, and our living becomes His living; this mingling produces a new creation (1 Cor. 6:17).
 F. If we would be in the new creation, we must enter into an organic union with the Triune God; apart from this union we remain in the old creation (2 Cor. 5:17).
 G. The new creation is the new man in Christ (Eph. 4:24), our being that is regenerated by the Spirit (John 3:6), having God's life and the divine nature wrought into it (v. 36; 2 Pet. 1:4), with Christ as its constituent (Col. 3:10-11); it is this new creation that fulfills God's eternal purpose by expressing God in His sonship.

Morning Nourishment

Eph. **That Christ may make His home in your hearts**
3:17 **through faith...**
Gal. **My children, with whom I travail again in birth**
4:19 **until Christ is formed in you.**
3:26 **For you are all sons of God through faith in Christ**
Jesus.

If we would know what it means for Christ to be formed in us, we need to consider not only the entire book of Galatians, but also the books of Ephesians, Philippians, and Colossians. The book of Galatians indicates that God's intention is for Christ to be wrought into His chosen people that they may become sons of God. In order to be God's sons, we need to be permeated and saturated with Christ. Christ must occupy our entire being. The Galatians, however, were distracted from Christ to the law. Hence, Paul told them repeatedly that it was altogether wrong to leave Christ and return to the law. The believers should come back to Christ, who is both the seed who fulfills God's promise to Abraham and also the good land, the all-inclusive Spirit to be our enjoyment. As believers, we need the full enjoyment of this blessing, the full enjoyment of the life-giving Spirit. We need to be permeated, saturated, possessed, and fully taken over by this Spirit and with this Spirit....To have Christ formed in us is to allow Him to permeate our being and to saturate our inward parts. When Christ occupies our inner being in this way, He is formed in us. (*Life-study of Galatians,* pp. 209-210)

Today's Reading

The most crucial and mysterious matter revealed in the Bible is that God's ultimate intention is to work Himself into His chosen people. God's desire to work Himself into our being is the focal point of the divine revelation in the Scriptures.

Throughout the centuries, Christians have not seen this matter clearly. Most readers of the Bible have paid their attention to many things other than this crucial and mysterious point in the divine revelation. We admit that it is not easy to see this crucial point in the Bible. Just as a person's physical life is mysterious and hidden within him, so it is with the matter of God's intention to work Himself into His chosen people. It is hidden in the Word. Life is the most vital element in a person's being. But who can analyze it or adequately explain it? With the Bible, as with a human being, there are many things that are outward and easily identified. But there is also a hidden element, which we may call the life factor in the Scriptures. We may say that this life factor is Christ or the Spirit. However, the life factor in the Bible is actually God's intention to work Himself into us. This is the kernel of the Bible.

Many theologians and Bible teachers have not seen the kernel of the Bible. In their writings they speak of many other things, but they do not mention this basic life factor. They have not pointed out definitely and particularly that according to the divine revelation in the Bible, God's intention is to work Himself into us. This is the reason that in the Lord's recovery we have given message after message on this point. Even after hundreds of messages have been given on the subject of God's intention, I still do not have the confidence that all the saints have an adequate understanding of it or that they have all truly seen it. I can testify that the vision of God's eternal intention has never been more clear to me than it is now. Throughout the years, this vision has become crystal clear. God's intention truly is to work Himself into us.

The book of Galatians is focused on Christ replacing the law. It is not God's intention to keep His people under the law. His intention is to dispense Christ into them. Thus, Christ as the center of God's economy must replace the law. Because the Judaizers were misusing the law, the Epistle to the Galatians was written to reveal Christ as the replacement of the law. Yes, the law was given for a specific purpose, but God did not intend for the law to be permanent. Christ has come to replace the law with Himself. This is the focal point of Galatians. (*Life-study of Galatians,* pp. 287-288, 309)

Further Reading: Life-study of Galatians, msgs. 24, 33, 35

Enlightenment and inspiration: _____

_____

_____

_____

Morning Nourishment

Gal. So then the law has become our child-conductor
3:24 unto Christ that we might be justified out of faith.
1:14-16 And I advanced in Judaism beyond many contemporaries in my race, being more abundantly a
zealot for the traditions of my fathers. But when it
pleased God...to reveal His Son in me...

In the book of Galatians God's two economies, His Old Testament economy and His New Testament economy, are dealt with in
a full way. Concerning each of these economies, the Bible uses a
particular word. The word for God's economy in the Old Testament
is *law,* and the word for His economy in the New Testament is
Christ. Which do you prefer, law or Christ? In contrast to the Jews,
who love the law, we who believe in Christ would all say that we
prefer Christ to the law. Yes, on the one hand, we do love Christ,
but, on the other hand, we may still embrace the law. In actual experience, we may embrace the law more than we embrace Christ.

Not many Christians have their daily walk according to Christ.
Can you say that you have been walking according to Christ today?...Whenever we do not live according to Christ, we live according to law. This is my reason for saying that although we love
Christ, we still hold to the law.

Our situation can be compared to that of Abraham, who loved
Sarah, his wife, but who also became involved with Hagar, a concu-
bine, who signifies the law....Hagar, the law, is within us, and we
love her. This law may not be the law of Moses. Instead, it may be
some type of self-made law. (*Life-study of Galatians,* pp. 363-364)

Today's Reading

[God's] first economy, the economy in the Old Testament, involves law, our ethical laws as well as the God-given law. Whenever
a person is regenerated, he continues to live according to the ethical laws he has assimilated from his culture. Very few, if any, live
Christ. Even though we may seek Christ, we still live our own cul-
tural laws and, thereby, in our actual experience, keep ourselves in
God's first economy.

The second economy of God, His New Testament economy, is
wholly related to Christ. Before Paul was converted, he was altogether in God's first economy. In 1:14 Paul tells us that he "advanced in Judaism beyond many contemporaries in my race, being
more abundantly a zealot for the traditions of my fathers." So zeal-
ous was he for the Jewish religion that he resolved to persecute all
those who were living in God's second economy. For this reason, he
"persecuted the church of God excessively and ravaged it" (1:13).
We are all familiar with the fact that when Paul was on the road to
Damascus, the Lord intervened and revealed Himself to Paul,
causing him to fall to the ground. Paul experienced a genuine conversion, a real turn from God's old economy of the law to His new
economy of Christ. He refers to this turn in 1:15 and 16, where he
tells us that it pleased God "to reveal His Son in me."

Christ was revealed not only to Paul, but also into him. When
Paul was a leading religionist, a "top dog" in Judaism, the Son of
God entered into him. This was the reason Paul says in 1:16 that
the Son of God was revealed in him, not merely to him. Because he
had such a revelation of Christ, Paul could testify to the believers,
"Dear saints, I want to tell you that I have the living person of the
Son of God within me. There is utterly no comparison between this
person and the law. The law is good, but it is inferior to this living
person. For years, I tried to keep the law. But one day the living person of the Son of God was revealed into me. What a wonder! What a
miracle!..."

What we see in chapter one of Galatians is a change of economy, a shift from the old economy to the new in which the Old
Testament economy is replaced by the New Testament economy.
This change is not a matter of theory, philosophy, or culture. It is
an actual shift related to the economy of God. Formerly, Paul was
absolutely given to God's Old Testament economy. But after Christ
was revealed into him, he was wholly in God's new economy.
(*Life-study of Galatians,* pp. 366-367)

Further Reading: Life-study of Galatians, msg. 41

Enlightenment and inspiration: _____

_____

_____

Morning Nourishment

Gal. But when the fullness of the time came, God sent
4:4-7 forth His Son, born of a woman, born under law,
that He might redeem those under law that we
might receive the sonship. And because you are
sons, God has sent forth the Spirit of His Son into
our hearts, crying, Abba, Father! So then you are
no longer a slave but a son; and if a son, an heir also
through God.

God's economy is to dispense Himself as the processed Triune God into our being to be our life and our everything, to make Himself one with us and us one with Him so that we may express Him in a corporate way for eternity. However, in the attempt to frustrate God's economy, Satan, the enemy of God, uses the law, which was given by God to serve His purpose temporarily, to keep God's chosen people from His economy and to distract them from it. If we look at the book of Galatians from this point of view, we shall find that it is not difficult to understand. As we read this Epistle, we need to see that God's economy is to impart Himself as the all-inclusive life-giving Spirit into us to produce an organic union between us and the Triune God so that we may express Him in a corporate way. But Satan utilizes the law given by God in order to distract God's people from His economy and to hinder the fulfillment of God's economy. (*Life-study of Galatians*, p. 137)

Today's Reading

God's chosen people were shut up by law under its custody (Gal. 3:23). Christ was born under law in order to redeem them from its custody that they might receive the sonship and become the sons of God. Hence, they should not return to the custody of law to be under its slavery as the Galatians had been seduced to do, but should remain in the sonship of God to enjoy the life supply of the Spirit in Christ. According to the entire revelation of the New Testament, God's economy is to produce sons. Sonship is the focal point of God's economy, God's dispensation. God's economy is the dispensation of Himself into His chosen people to make them His sons. Christ's redemption is to bring us into the sonship of God that we may enjoy the divine life. It is not God's economy to make us keepers of law, obeying the commandments and ordinances of the law, which was given only for a temporary purpose. God's economy is to make us sons of God, inheriting the blessing of God's promise, which was given for His eternal purpose. His eternal purpose is to have many sons for His corporate expression (Heb. 2:10; Rom. 8:29). Hence, He predestinated us unto sonship (Eph. 1:5) and regenerated us to be His sons (John 1:12-13). We should remain in His sonship that we may become His heirs to inherit all He has planned for His eternal expression, and should not be distracted to Judaism by the appreciation of law.

It is difficult to give an adequate definition of sonship. Sonship involves life, maturity, position, and privilege. To be a son of the Father, we need to have the Father's life. However, we must go on to mature in this life. Life and maturity give us the right, the privilege, the position, to inherit the things of the Father. According to the New Testament, sonship includes life, maturity, position, and right.

It is not God's intention simply to have a group of good people; He wants many sons who are one with Him organically and who possess His very life and nature. Only these sons can be members of the Body of Christ. The Body of Christ is an organism, not an organization. Good people may be organized into a society, but they cannot become the organism known as the Body of Christ. Because the Body is organic, all the members of the Body must have an organic element in them. We receive this element by the new birth, by regeneration. (*Life-study of Galatians,* pp. 191-192, 395)

Further Reading: Life-study of Galatians, msgs. 16, 22, 44

Enlightenment and inspiration: _____

_____

_____

_____

Morning Nourishment

Gal. I am crucified with Christ; and *it is* no longer I *who*
2:20 live, but *it is* Christ *who* lives in me...
  3:3 Are you so foolish? Having begun by the Spirit, are
       you now being perfected by the flesh?
 6:14 But far be it from me to boast except in the cross of
       our Lord Jesus Christ, through whom the world has
       been crucified to me and I to the world.
Phil. For to me, to live is Christ...
1:21

The book of Galatians shows that Paul was an excellent
writer. After so much argument and debate in chapter three,
Paul concludes by saying that we have been baptized into
Christ, that we have put on Christ, and that we are all one
in Christ. We who have the hearing of faith have been put
into Christ. Now we need to live Christ and express Christ. This
will cause us to be one in Christ in the church life.

The Galatian believers were foolish in going back to the law.
Paul seemed to be telling them, "You have all been baptized into
Christ and into the one Body. Now you should take Christ as
your clothing, your expression, and live Him. Don't go back to
the law to try to fulfill its requirements. Stay with Christ and
live out Christ. Remember, you are members of the one Body, of
the one new man. Stay with all those who are in Christ, and
practice the church life so that God's purpose can be fulfilled. If
you go back to the law, you will be in slavery again. The desire of
God's heart cannot be satisfied by your efforts to keep the law. It
can be satisfied only if you remain with Christ and live Him out."
Praise the Lord that we have entered into an organic union with
Him and that now we are living Christ in the church, the one
Body. Surely this satisfies God. (*Life-study of Galatians*, p. 189)

Today's Reading

Christ, the Spirit, the new creation, and our spirit are the
four basic things revealed in this book as the underlying thought
of God's economy. Christ is the center of God's economy, and the
Spirit is the reality of Christ. When Christ is realized through

the Spirit in our spirit, we become the new creation. Thus, our spirit is vital for us to live the life of the new creation for the fulfilling of God's purpose.

The book of Galatians places a strong emphasis on the cross and on the experience of crucifixion. Then, on the positive side, this book reveals Christ, the Spirit, the sons of God, the heirs of promise, the household of faith, the new creation, and the Israel of God. As we have seen, in 6:18 Paul refers to our spirit. On the negative side, the book of Galatians speaks of the law, the flesh, the "I," the religious world, slavery, and the curse. However, the three main items of the negative things dealt with in Galatians are the law, the flesh, and religion. These three things go together. When we are under the law, we are involved with both the flesh and religion. The religion in Galatians is the highest religion, the Hebrew religion formed according to God's oracle. Nevertheless, even this religion is related to the law and the flesh. By the cross we are set free from the law, the flesh, and religion, and we have Christ, the Spirit, the new creation, and our regenerated spirit. If we see this vision, we shall praise the Lord for the cross. Because of the cross of Christ, the law, the flesh, and religion have all been terminated. But through the cross of Christ we have the Spirit, the new creation, and our spirit. Now, by the Spirit, who is the realization of Christ in our spirit, we may live the new creation. Living the new creation, we bear the brands of Jesus and enjoy the grace of the Lord Jesus Christ in our spirit. With Paul we can say, "Let no one trouble me, for I bear in my body the brands of Jesus." Then we shall know that the grace of Christ is with our spirit. This is the way Paul concludes the book of Galatians. (*Life-study of Galatians,* pp. 276-277)

Further Reading: Life-study of Galatians, msgs. 1, 6, 8, 22, 24, 27, 35, 40; *A General Sketch of the New Testament in the Light of Christ and the Church, Part 2: Romans through Philemon,* ch. 15; *Life-study of Psalms,* msg. 8

Enlightenment and inspiration: _____

_____

_____

_____

Morning Nourishment

Gal. Paul, an apostle (not from men nor through man
1:1 but through Jesus Christ and God the Father, who
raised Him from the dead).
6:15 For neither is circumcision anything nor uncircumcision, but a new creation *is what matters.*
Eph. And put on the new man, which was created ac-
4:24 cording to God in righteousness and holiness of
the reality.

The purpose of the book of Galatians is to let those who receive it know that the gospel preached by the apostle Paul was
not from man's teaching (1:11), but from God's revelation.
Hence, at the very opening of this book [v. 1], Paul emphasized
the fact that he became an apostle not from men nor through
man but through Christ and God.

Paul is careful in his use of words....He was made an apostle
directly through Jesus Christ and God the Father, who raised
Christ from among the dead. The law dealt with man as the old
creation, whereas the gospel makes man the new creation in
resurrection. God made Paul an apostle not according to his natural man in the old creation by the law, but according to his regenerated man in the new creation through the resurrection of
Christ....God's New Testament economy is not with man in the
old creation but with man in the new creation through the resurrection of Christ. Paul's apostleship belonged altogether to the
new creation, which transpires in our spirit through regeneration by the Spirit of God. (*Life-study of Galatians,* p. 10)

Today's Reading

In Galatians 6:15 Paul says that neither circumcision nor
uncircumcision is anything, but a new creation. The old creation
is our old man in Adam (Eph. 4:22), our natural being by birth,
without God's life and the divine nature. The new creation is the
new man in Christ (Eph. 4:24), our being regenerated by the
Spirit (John 3:6), having God's life and the divine nature

wrought into us (John 3:36; 2 Pet. 1:4), with Christ as its constituent (Col. 3:10-11). It is this new creation that fulfills God's eternal purpose by expressing God in His sonship.

Circumcision is an ordinance of law; the new creation is the
masterpiece of life with the divine nature. The former is of dead
letters; the latter is of the living Spirit. Hence, it counts, it avails.
This book exposes the inability both of the law and of circumcision. Law cannot impart life (Gal. 3:21) to regenerate us, and circumcision cannot energize us (5:6) to live a new creation. But the
Son of God who has been revealed in us (1:16) can enliven us and
make us a new creation, and Christ who lives in us (2:20) can afford
us the riches of His life to live the new creation. Law is replaced by
Christ (2:19-20), and circumcision is fulfilled by Christ's crucifixion (6:14). Hence, neither is circumcision anything nor uncircumcision, but a new creation with Christ as its life.

The new creation spoken of in 6:15 is the old creation transformed by the divine life, by the processed Triune God. The old
creation was old because God was not part of it; the new creation is new because God is in it. We who have been regenerated by the Spirit of God are still God's creation, but we are
now His new creation. However, this is real only when we live
and walk by the Spirit. Whenever we live and walk by the
flesh, we are in the old creation, not in the new creation. Anything in our daily life that does not have God in it is the old
creation, but what has God in it is part of the new creation.

God's intention is that we become a new creation. This new
creation is composed of sons. In a very practical sense, the corporate sonship is God's new creation. Those in the old creation are
sons of Adam in the fall. But through God's redemption and regeneration and through the dispensation of Himself into us, we
who once were sons of Adam have now become sons of God. Here
in this divine sonship we are the new creation. (*Life-study of
Galatians,* pp. 265-266)

Further Reading: Life-study of Galatians, msgs. 1, 30

Enlightenment and inspiration: _____

_____

_____

_____

Morning Nourishment

Gal. For neither is circumcision anything nor uncir-
6:15 cumcision, but a new creation *is what matters.*
1 John Whoever confesses that Jesus is the Son of God,
4:15 God abides in him and he in God.
2 Cor. So then if anyone is in Christ, *he is* a new creation.
5:17 The old things have passed away; behold, they
have become new.

Another aspect of the truth of the gospel is that in Christ man
is to be a new creation [Gal. 6:15]....The new creation is the mingling of God with man. The new creation takes place when the
Triune God in Christ through the Spirit is wrought into our being. This is the mingling of divinity with humanity. Living in this
new creation far surpasses trying to keep the law. How foolish
the Galatian believers were in going back to the law! They
should remain in Christ by faith. In this union with Christ,
Christ lives in us, and we become a new creation. Although we
remain God's creature, we are nonetheless mingled with God
the Creator. Having become one with the Creator, His life becomes our life, and our living becomes His living. This mingling
produces a new creation. This is not accomplished by works of
law, but by faith in Christ. (*Life-study of Galatians,* p. 76)

Today's Reading

If we would be in the new creation, we must enter into an organic union with the Triune God. Apart from such a union, we
shall remain in the old creation. But now by the organic union
with the Triune God we are in the new creation...[where] neither
circumcision nor uncircumcision is anything or avails anything.

Apparently Paul wrote the book of Galatians to deal with the
law. Actually this book deals with the old creation. Although
Paul tells us that we are justified by faith, the main point is not
justification, but the new creation. When we were in the flesh,
we were very much involved with the law and we were, of course,
in the old creation. But when we are in the Spirit, we are not

under the law and we are in the new creation. Thus, Paul's concern in Galatians is not merely with the doctrine concerning the law and justification by faith; it is with the revelation that we are God's new creation. Here we are no longer involved with law-keeping, circumcision, and religious practices. In the new creation only one thing is vital and crucial to us—the Triune God who has been processed to become the life-giving Spirit so that He may be our life, our nature, and our everything through the organic union between us and Him. How wonderful it is that in this organic union we are a new creation!

Many readers of Galatians have missed this crucial point. They have seen that in this Epistle the law is set aside and that justification by faith is emphasized. But Paul's burden in this book is not merely justification by faith; it is to unveil to his readers the matter of sonship by the divine life, by the Triune God becoming everything to us in our experience. When considered corporately, the sons of God are the new creation. The main issue in Galatians is not circumcision or uncircumcision, religion or no religion. It is an issue of whether or not we are the new creation through an organic union with the Triune God.

If we would live the new creation, we need to experience the cross. According to 6:14 and 15, the cross deals with the religious world. It is unfortunate that many Christians regard the world in 6:14 as only the secular world. But as we have already indicated, the context makes it clear that the world in this verse is primarily the religious world. This understanding fits the basic concept of the whole book of Galatians. This book was written not to deal with the secular world; it was written to deal with religion, with Judaism. In this book Paul deals with religious people, with those who are concerned for the things of God, but who express their concern in a wrong way. To them, religion has become a world. Hence, we have both the secular world and the religious world. (*Life-study of Galatians*, pp. 266-267)

Further Reading: Life-study of Galatians, msgs. 1, 8, 30

Enlightenment and inspiration: _____

_____

_____

_____

Hymns, #541

1   Not the law of letters,
  But the Christ of life
  God desires to give us,
  Saving us from strife;
  It is not some doctrine,
  But 'tis Christ Himself
  Who alone releases
  From our sinful self.

2   Any kind of teaching,
  Any kind of form,
  Cannot quicken spirits
  Or our souls transform;
  It is Christ as Spirit
  Gives us life divine,
  Thus thru us to live the
  Life of God's design.

3   Not philosophy nor
  Any element
  Can to Christ conform us
  As His complement;
  But 'tis Christ Himself who
  All our nature takes
  And in resurrection
  Us His members makes.

4   Not religion, even
  Christianity,
  Can fulfill God's purpose
  Or economy;
  But 'tis Christ within us
  As our all in all
  Satisfies God's wishes,
  And His plan withal.

5   All the gifts we're given
  By the Lord in grace,
  All the different functions
  Cannot Christ replace.
  Only Christ Himself must
  Be our all in all!
  Only Christ Himself in
  All things, great or small!

Composition for prophecy with main point and sub-points: _____

_____

_____

_____

_____

_____

_____

_____

_____

_____

_____

_____

_____

_____

_____

_____

_____

_____

_____

_____

_____

_____

_____

_____

_____

_____

_____

_____

_____

_____

**Being Rescued out of the Present Evil Age
by the Revelation of God's Son in Us**

Scripture Reading: Gal. 1:3-4, 11-16

Day 1
**I. The subject of the book of Galatians is the
rescue of the distracted believers out of the
evil religious age (1:3-4):**

A. An age refers to a section, an aspect, the present
or modern appearance, of the world as the satanic system, which is used by Satan to usurp
and occupy God's people to keep them away
from God and His purpose (Eph. 2:2; 1 John
2:14-15).

B. According to the context of this book, the present evil age here refers to the religious world,
the religious course of the world, the Jewish religion, which became formal in letter, deadening
in quenching the Spirit, killing in man's com-
munication with God in life, and contending
with the gospel of Christ in God's New Testament economy (Gal. 6:14-15; 1:6-16; 2 Cor. 3:6;
Phil. 3:2-3).

Day 2
C. The purpose of Christ's giving Himself for our
sins was to rescue us, to pluck us, out of the Jewish religion, the present evil age; this is to release God's chosen people from the custody of
the law (Gal. 3:23), to bring them out of the
sheepfold (John 10:1, 3, 16), according to the will
of God (cf. 1 Tim. 1:3-4):

1. According to the revelation of the typology
in the Song of Songs, Christ leads His lov-
ing seeker into her spirit, and in her spirit
in fellowship with Him, she receives the
revelation of how to leave the place where
she is kept away from the church to go forth
on the footsteps of the flock (1:4b-8).

2. The flock is the church as the place where

Christ pastures, shepherds and feeds, His
saints (John 10:16; Acts 20:28; 1 Pet. 5:2).

3. The Lord's seeker was seeking after the
Lord for her own satisfaction, but the
Lord's concern for His saved sinners is not
just for their satisfaction but for God's eternal economy; God's economy is to save sinners to gain the churches so that the
essence of these churches can become the
organic Body of Christ as the precursor for
the consummation of the New Jerusalem
(Rom. 5:10; Rev. 1:11-12; Eph. 1:22-23; Rev.
19:7-9; 21:2).

Day 3   D. We must overcome the present evil age of today's degraded Christendom with its Judaistic
system by holding to the teaching of the apostles
(the New Testament) through the all-inclusive
life-giving Spirit (Acts 2:42; 1 Tim. 1:3-4):

1. Judaism has earthly promises with earthly
blessings, but in the new testament we
have the all-inclusive Spirit as the totality
of the unsearchable riches of Christ to be
our unique blessing for us to bless others to
issue in the fullness of God (Gen. 12:2-3;
Gal. 3:14; Eph. 3:8; 1:3; Luke 12:21; Rev. 2:9;
2 Cor. 6:10; Eph. 3:19b).

2. Judaism has the law of letters, but in the new
testament we have the law of the Spirit of life
(Rom. 8:2; Heb. 8:10; Rom. 2:28-29; 5:20).

3. Judaism has mediatorial priests, but in the
new testament all the believers are priests
to be a holy and royal priesthood (Rev.
1:5b-6; 1 Pet. 2:5, 9; cf. Rev. 2:6).

4. Judaism has a material temple, but in the
new testament the temple is a spiritual
house, a dwelling place of God in spirit
(Eph. 2:21-22):

a. In Judaism the worshippers and the
place of worship are two different things,

but in the new testament the place of
worship is the worshipper (John 4:24;
Acts 2:46; 5:42).

 b. The Father's house, typified by the temple, is a divine and human incorporation
of the processed and consummated God
constituted with His redeemed, regenerated, and transformed elect (John 14:2,
20, 23; 1 Tim. 3:15; Rev. 21:3, 22).

Day 4 II. **God's Son is versus man's religion (Gal.
1:11-16):**

A. The desire of God's heart is to reveal His Son in
us that we may know Him, receive Him as our
life (John 17:3; 3:16), and become the sons of
God (1:12; Gal. 4:5-6).

B. The focal point of the Bible is not practices, doctrines, or ordinances—it is the living person of
the Son of God, who is the embodiment of the
Triune God realized as the all-inclusive Spirit in
our spirit for us to enjoy Him, partake of His
riches, and live Him (1 Cor. 15:45b; 2 Cor. 3:17;
Phil. 1:19; Gal. 6:18):

1. In the eyes of God, there is no place for religion or tradition—only the living person of
His Son has a place; God cares only for this
living person, not for anything else (Col.
1:18b; 2:16-17; 3:10b-11; Mark 9:7-8).

2. Without this living person as the reality
and content of the church life, even the
church life will become a tradition; the
church is the Body of this person, His fullness, His practical and living expression
(Eph. 1:22-23; 3:8-11, 16-19).

Day 5 III. **Nothing is more pleasing to God than the unveiling, the revelation, of the living person
of the Son of God in us (Gal. 1:15a, 16a; 2 Cor.
3:14-17; 4:3-6):**

A. The more inward, subjective revelation we receive of the Son of God, the more He will live in

us; the more He lives in us, the more He will become to us the reality of the all-inclusive land as the blessing of Abraham, the blessing of the all-inclusive life-giving Spirit (Gal. 2:20; 3:14).

Day 6

B. If we drop our concepts, turn our heart to the Lord, pay attention to the spirit, and spend time in the Word in a spirit and atmosphere of prayer, Christ will be revealed in us, live in us, and be formed in us (1:15-16; 2:20; 4:19):

1. We must drop our concepts; every concept, whether spiritual or carnal, is a veil; this inward revelation is in our spirit through our enlightened mind (2 Cor. 3:14-15; 4:4; Eph. 1:17-18; Luke 24:45).

2. We must turn our heart to the Lord; the more we turn our heart to the Lord, the less ground the god of this age will have in our life and in our being, and we will be under the shining of the heavenly light to receive the inward revelation of this living person (2 Cor. 3:16, 18).

3. We must care for and pay attention to our spirit; it is in our spirit that the Spirit is shining, revealing Christ in us, and speaking to us concerning Christ (Eph. 1:17; 3:5; cf. Rev. 1:10; 2:7).

4. We must pray-read the Word (Eph. 6:17-18).

C. We need to be full of the revelation of the Son of God and thereby become a new creation with Christ living in us, being formed in us, and being enjoyed by us continually as the all-inclusive Spirit (Gal. 6:14-15).

Morning Nourishment

Gal. Who gave Himself for our sins that He might res-
1:4 cue us out of the present evil age according to the
     will of our God and Father.
John To him the doorkeeper opens, and the sheep hear
10:3 his voice; and he calls his own sheep by name and
     leads them out.
16   And I have other sheep, which are not of this fold; I
     must lead them also, and they shall hear My voice,
     and there shall be one flock, one Shepherd.

The subject of the book of Galatians is related to its background. The subject is the rescue of the distracted believers out of the evil religious age [1:4]….An age is a part of the world as the satanic system. An age refers to a section, an aspect, the present or modern appearance, of the system of Satan, which is used by him to usurp and occupy people and keep them away from God and His purpose.

The present evil age in 1:4, according to the context of this book, refers to the religious world, the religious course of the world, the Jewish religion. This is confirmed by 6:14-15, where circumcision is considered a part of the world—the religious world which to the apostle Paul is crucified. Here the apostle emphasizes that the purpose of Christ's giving Himself for our sins was to rescue us, to pluck us out, from the Jewish religion, the present evil age. This is to release God's chosen people from the custody of the law (3:23), to bring them out of the sheepfold (John 10:1, 3), according to the will of God. Thus, in his opening word, Paul indicates what he is about to deal with. He desires to rescue the churches which were distracted by Judaism with its law and to bring them back to the grace of the gospel. (*Life-study of Galatians,* pp. 7-8)

Today's Reading

In Galatians 1:4 Paul points out that in order to rescue us from the present evil religious age Christ gave Himself for our sins. This indicates that Christ died in order to rescue us from Judaism. In John 10 we see that Christ as the good Shepherd entered into the fold in order to bring His sheep out of the fold and into the pasture. The fold in John 10 signifies the law or Judaism as the religion of the law, in which God's chosen people were kept and guarded in custody or ward until Christ came. Before the coming of Christ, God used Judaism as a fold to keep His sheep. But Christ has come as the Shepherd to bring the sheep out of that fold to the pasture where they may feed on His riches. Although Christ came to release the sheep from the fold, the Judaizers crucified this good Shepherd. He died on the cross not only for the sins of the sheep, but also to bring them out of the fold.

We should apply Galatians 1:4 not only to the Galatian believers, but also to today's believers in Christ. Most Christians are held in some kind of religious fold....In principle, Catholicism and all the denominations are folds. Only the church is God's flock. Christ has brought us back to the flock, not to the fold. Many of us can testify that we have been rescued out of the fold and brought back to God's flock.

At the time of John 10, God's people, His sheep, were in the fold of Judaism. But as this chapter makes clear, Christ came to bring His sheep out of the fold and to form them with the Gentile believers into one flock, the church (10:16). Hence, the fold is religion, whereas the flock is the church. Today Catholicism and the denominations are folds that keep Christ's sheep. But Christ is seeking to rescue His sheep out of the various religious folds and to bring them together as the one flock.

The Lord Jesus came into the fold, opened the door, and led the sheep out of the fold. The Judaizers crucified Him. But through His death on the cross, the Lord gave Himself for our sins in order to rescue us from the religious fold. The principle is the same both with the believers in Paul's time and with us today. (*Life-study of Galatians,* pp. 8-10)

Further Reading: Life-study of Galatians, msg. 1; *Elders' Training, Book 6: The Crucial Points of the Truth in Paul's Epistles,* ch. 5; *The Indwelling Christ in the Canons of the New Testament,* ch. 11

Enlightenment and inspiration: _____

_____

_____

Morning Nourishment

S. S.   ...My mother's sons were angry with me; they made
1:6-8   me keeper of the vineyards, *but* my own vineyard I
         have not kept. Tell me, you whom my soul loves,
         where do you pasture *your flock?* Where do you
         make *it* lie down at noon? For why should I be like
         one who is veiled beside the flocks of your compan-
         ions? If you yourself do not know, you fairest among
         women, go forth on the footsteps of the flock...
John   And I have other sheep, which are not of this fold; I
10:16   must lead them also, and they shall hear My voice,
        and there shall be one flock, one Shepherd.

In the Lord's care for His seeker [in the Song of Songs], the
Lord was very wise. She was seeking after the Lord for her own
satisfaction. That was her concern. But the Lord's concern with
His saved sinners is not just for their satisfaction but for God's
eternal economy. Thus, the concerns are different. Our concern
is very low, personal, but the Lord's concern is God's economy.
God's economy is to save sinners to gain the churches, so that the
essence of these churches can become the organic Body of Christ
for the consummation of the New Jerusalem. The Lord's intention in saving us is for us to be in the church so that we can be
built up in the Body of Christ and be in the consummation of
God's economy, the New Jerusalem. (*Crystallization-study of
Song of Songs*, p. 23)

Today's Reading

Many do not even like to talk about the church because of
all the complications and confusion with the denominations. The
seeker says that her mother's sons were angry with her. The
mother signifies grace as the one who begot the seeker and her
brothers (cf. Gal. 4:26). Her brothers born of the same grace persecuted her and pressed her to work in the vineyards while she
neglected her own vineyard. Song of Songs 1:7 speaks of the flocks
of the Lord's companions. These flocks turn the seeker away from

the Lord's presence. As a result the seeker says to the Lord, "Where do you pasture your flock? / Where do you make it lie down at noon?" The companions are the Lord's companions, but their flocks are not His flock. Their flocks carried the seeker away from Christ Himself and from His feeding and shepherding.

All the founders of the denominations are Christ's companions, His friends....They were Christ's companions who went out for Christ, but not to set up the churches of Christ. They were very good with respect to Christ, but they did something wrong with respect to the church life, because they set up their own flocks. Such companions of the Lord were positive, but unintentionally they established flocks which separated Christ's real seekers from His presence with His shepherding and feeding.

Our experience was that the more we stayed in the denominations, the more we lost the Lord's presence. We left the denominations because we lost the presence of Christ. In the hardships, at noontime, we did not enjoy the shepherding of Christ. Christ was not with us, so we did not have rest and satisfaction. One day we met the Lord's recovery and found out that, although it was not perfect, it was the highest place. The church is the place where Christ pastures, shepherds, and feeds His saints. We left the denominations because we had no rest, no satisfaction, and no real enjoyment of Christ. We may have been saved in a denomination, and that denomination may have helped us, taught us, and built us up to know Christ to a certain extent, but it was also that denomination which hindered us from going on to enjoy Christ with His rest and satisfaction. In today's confusion of the divisions in Christianity, we should realize where to go. All of the Lord's seekers should follow the footsteps of His flock.

The Lord instructed His seeker to follow the footsteps of the flock, which are the footsteps of all the faithful Christ-seekers throughout the centuries. (*Crystallization-study of Song of Songs*, pp. 23-25)

Further Reading: Crystallization-study of Song of Songs, msg. 2

Enlightenment and inspiration: _____

_____

_____

Morning Nourishment

John God is Spirit, and those who worship Him must
4:24 worship in spirit and truthfulness.
Eph. In whom you also are being built together into a
2:22 dwelling place of God in spirit.
Rom. For the law of the Spirit of life has freed me in
8:2   Christ Jesus from the law of sin and of death.
1 Pet. But you are a chosen race, a royal priesthood, a
2:9   holy nation...

There are many essential differences between Judaism and the church. Here I wish to mention four points to which we must give special attention: the temple, the law, the priests, and the promises. As their place of worship, the Jews built a splendid temple on this earth of stone and gold. As their standard of behavior, they have the Ten Commandments and many other regulations. In order to attend to spiritual affairs, they have the office of the priests, a group of special people. Finally, they also have the blessings by which they may prosper on this earth. Please notice that Judaism is an earthly religion on this earth. They have a material temple, regulations of letters, mediatorial priests, and enjoyment on this earth. (Watchman Nee, *The Orthodoxy of the Church*, p. 24)

Today's Reading

When the Jews entered the land of Canaan, they built the temple....This is called the place of worship. The Jews are worshippers, and the temple is the place where they worship. The worshippers and the place of worship are two different things. But is this so in the New Testament? The special feature of the church is that there is no place and no temple, because we, the people, are the temple.

The special feature of the church is that your body is the dwelling place of God. Individually speaking, every one of us is the temple of God. Corporately speaking, God builds us up and fits us together to become His dwelling place [Eph. 2:21-22]. There is no place of worship in the church; the place of worship is the worshipper....This is basically different from Judaism. The temple in Judaism is a material temple; the temple in the church is a spiritual temple.

The Jews also have laws and regulations for their daily life (God only uses the law to make men know their sins). Whoever is a Jew must keep the Ten Commandments....Judaism has a standard of principles for daily living which is written on tablets of stone....The daily-living standard of Judaism is dead; it is something outward. In the church there is no law; rather, its law is in another place. It is not written on tablets of stone but on tablets of the heart. The law of the Spirit of life is within us. The Holy Spirit dwells in us; the Holy Spirit is our law....Today our special feature is that the Spirit of God dwells in us.

Today's Christianity has already been Judaized....The fathers, clergymen, and pastors undertake the spiritual things for everyone....Whenever the church comes to the point of having only a handful of people undertake the spiritual things, that church has already fallen....The church demands that we offer our whole body to God. This is the only way. Everyone must be serving the Lord.

The purpose of the Jews in serving God is that they may reap more....They are after blessings in this world....But the first promise to the church is that we must take up the cross and follow the Lord....The church does not teach how much we shall gain before God, but how much we will be able to let go before God. The church does not think that suffering is a painful thing; rather, it is a joy. Today these four items—the material temple, the outward laws, the mediatorial priests, and the worldly promises—are in the church. Brothers and sisters, we desire to preach the word of God more. We hope that all the children of God, even though they have secular occupations, will be spiritual men. (Watchman Nee, *The Orthodoxy of the Church,* pp. 24-28)

Further Reading: The Orthodoxy of the Church, ch. 3; The Overcomers, ch. 4

Enlightenment and inspiration: _____

_____

_____

_____

Morning Nourishment

Gal. For you have heard of my manner of life formerly in
1:13-16 Judaism, that I persecuted the church of God excessively and ravaged it. And I advanced in Judaism beyond many contemporaries in my race, being
more abundantly a zealot for the traditions of my
fathers. But when it pleased God, who set me apart
from my mother's womb and called me through His
grace, to reveal His Son in me that I might announce Him as the gospel among the Gentiles...

The Son of God as the embodiment and expression of God the
Father (John 1:18; 14:9-11; Heb. 1:3) is life to us (John 10:10;
1 John 5:12; Col. 3:4). The desire of God's heart is to reveal His
Son in us that we may know Him, receive Him as our life (John
17:3; 3:16), and become the sons of God (John 1:12; Gal. 4:5-6). As
the Son of the living God (Matt. 16:16), Christ is far superior to
Judaism and its traditions (Gal. 1:13-14). The Judaizers be-
witched the Galatians so that they considered the ordinances of
the law above the Son of the living God. Hence, the apostle in the
opening of this Epistle testified that he had been deeply involved
in that realm and far advanced in it. God, however, had rescued
him out of that course of the world, which was evil in God's eyes,
by revealing His Son in him. In his experience, Paul realized
that there is no comparison between the Son of the living God
and Judaism with its dead traditions from his fathers.
(*Life-study of Galatians,* p. 22)

Today's Reading

It is significant that in Galatians 1:15 and 16 Paul does not
say that God revealed Christ in him, but that He revealed His
Son in him....Whenever we speak of the Son of God, we are immediately involved with the Father and the Spirit. According to
the writings of Paul, to have the Son is to have both the Father
and the Spirit....The Son is the embodiment of the Triune God
realized as the Spirit for our enjoyment. Hence, when Paul says

that it pleased God to reveal His Son in him, this means that the One revealed in him was the embodiment of the Triune God realized as the processed all-inclusive Spirit. The burden I have received from the Lord is to minister this matter to God's chosen people. Although I have been ministering on this for many years, I can testify that this burden is heavier today than ever before.

In Paul's Epistles we see that the Son is the mystery of God, the embodiment of God, and the One in whom the fullness of the Godhead dwells bodily (Col. 2:2, 9). One day, through incarnation, the Son of God became a man called the last Adam, who, through death and resurrection, has become the life-giving Spirit (1 Cor. 15:45). In 2 Corinthians 3:17 Paul says, "Now the Lord is the Spirit." Putting all these verses together, we see that the Son of God, the embodiment of the fullness of the Godhead, became a man and that in resurrection this One is now the life-giving Spirit.

However, because of the fall, we are easily distracted to care for other things in place of Christ....[Therefore], it is crucial for us to have a vision of this all-inclusive living person. This person includes the Father, the Son, and the Spirit; He includes divinity and humanity. Although this living person is so all-inclusive, He is very practical to us, for, as the life-giving Spirit, He is in our regenerated spirit. On the one hand, He is in the heavens as the Lord, the Christ, the King, the Head, the High Priest, and the heavenly Minister; on the other hand, He is in our spirit to be everything to us. He is God, the Father, the Redeemer, the Savior, man, life, light, and the reality of every positive thing. This is the living person of the Son of God.

We need to pray that we shall care for this living person more than anything, even more than for the church life. Without this living person as the reality and content of the church life, even the church life will become a tradition. Oh, it is vital that we see this living person! (*Life-study of Galatians,* pp. 27-29)

Further Reading: Life-study of Galatians, msg. 3

Enlightenment and inspiration: _____

_____

_____

Do you want to please God?
Allow Him to reveal His Son in you

Morning Nourishment

Gal. But when it pleased God...to reveal His Son in me,...
1:15-16 immediately I did not confer with flesh and blood.

2:20 I am crucified with Christ; and *it is* no longer I *who* live, but *it is* Christ *who* lives in me...

4:19 My children, with whom I travail again in birth until Christ is formed in you.

Eph. That the God of our Lord Jesus Christ, the Father of
1:17 glory, may give to you a spirit of wisdom and revelation in the full knowledge of Him.

Only people who live in spirit can be wise.
Wisdom is for revelation

In Galatians 1:15 and 16 Paul says that it pleased God to reveal His Son in him. This indicates that to reveal the Son of God brings pleasure to God. Nothing is more pleasing to God than the unveiling, the revelation, of the living person of the Son of God. *—that we may see Him clearly* Furthermore, this revelation is an inward revelation. Although I have never seen the Lord Jesus outwardly in a physical way, I have seen Him inwardly. I have received an inward revelation of this living person. This inward revelation is in our spirit through our enlightened mind. Because the mind plays an important part, it is crucial that we drop our concepts, all of which are in the mind. If we hold on to concepts in our mind, the revelation may be in our spirit, but it will not be able to penetrate our veiled mentality. We need to drop our concepts so that our mind may be released and become transparent. Then when the Spirit shines in our spirit, this shining will come into our transparent mind. Then we shall receive an inward revelation. (*Life-study of Galatians*, pp. 38-39)

not baffled by many fixed concepts

Today's Reading

This inward revelation of Christ is subjective....This subjective revelation is given in our spirit by the Spirit (Eph. 1:17; 3:5). Our spirit and the Spirit of God both are realities. We cannot deny that within us we have a human spirit. Neither can we deny that the divine Spirit is in our spirit. In order to receive the revelation of the Son of God, we must first drop our concepts.

greatly appreciate

Second, we must turn our hearts to the Lord and worship nothing other than Him. Third, we must take care of the depths of our being, that is, of our spirit. It is in our spirit that the Spirit is shining, revealing Christ in us and speaking to us concerning Christ. It is also helpful to pray-read the Word, especially verses from the Epistles of Paul. This will enable us to see Christ and to receive a subjective revelation of this living person.

The subjective revelation about which we are speaking here is concerned only with the living person of the Son of God. For the sake of receiving such a revelation, may we all learn to drop our concepts, to turn our heart to the Lord, to pay attention to our spirit, and to pray over verses from the writings of Paul. Then the Spirit will enlighten us and speak to us of Christ. As a result, we shall receive a subjective revelation of the Son of God.

The more revelation we receive of the Son of God, the more He will live in us. The more He lives in us, the more He will become to us the unique and central blessing of the gospel which God promised to Abraham. This means that He will be to us the all-inclusive land realized as the all-inclusive, processed life-giving Spirit. This should not simply be a doctrine to us. If we drop our concepts, turn our heart to the Lord, pay attention to the spirit, and spend time in the Word, Christ will be revealed in us, He will live in us, and He will be formed in us. Day by day, He will become more of an enjoyment to us. As a result, this living person will make us a new creation in a practical way. The book of Galatians eventually brings us to the new creation by way of the inward revelation of the living person of the Son of God.

Not a matter of trying but of seeing

Paul's burden in writing the book of Galatians, and our need today, is that we be brought into a state where we are full of the revelation of the Son of God and thereby become a new creation with Christ living in us, being formed in us, and being enjoyed by us continually as the all-inclusive Spirit. (*Life-study of Galatians*, pp. 39-40)

Further Reading: Life-study of Galatians, msg. 4

Enlightenment and inspiration: _____

_____

_____

[handwritten: the OT Scriptures]

Morning Nourishment

**2 Cor. Indeed unto this day, whenever Moses is read, a
3:15-16 veil lies on their heart; but whenever *their heart*
turns to the Lord, the veil is taken away.**

[handwritten: This age has its blinding thoughts]

**4:3-4 And even if our gospel is veiled, it is veiled in those
who are perishing, in whom the god of this age has
blinded the thoughts of the unbelievers that the illumination of the gospel of the glory of Christ, who
is the image of God, might not shine on them.**

[handwritten: into them]

Let us daily practice receiving revelation by dropping our concepts and turning our hearts to the Lord. The way to receive an
inward, subjective, spiritual revelation is always to drop our concepts, to turn our heart to the Lord, and to tell the Lord that we
hold on to nothing besides Him and that our heart is wholly for
Him. Then if we pay attention to our spirit and spend time in the
Word, we shall receive revelation. The living person will live in us
and be formed in us. We shall enjoy Him more and more, and He
will make us a new creation. (*Life-study of Galatians,* p. 40)

Today's Reading

With respect to receiving revelation, there is no problem on
God's side. On His side everything is ready. The problem is altogether on our side. We need to drop the veils, that is, to drop our
concepts....If you hold on to your concepts while reading the Bible, you will be like the ancient Jews who had a veil on their
mind whenever the Scriptures were read. But if you drop your
concepts as you read the Word, you will read it with an unveiled
face. Then the light will shine into you subjectively.

I was born into Christianity, and from childhood I heard about
Christ. However, I was not saved until I was nineteen years old. I
knew about Jesus, and I was in favor of Christianity. But I was not
saved until the Son of God was revealed in me. One day, when I
was nineteen, God shined into me, and I received a revelation of
the Lord Jesus. At that time I began to have direct personal contact with Him and to know Him as a living person. I touched Him,
and I was touched by Him. Between Him and me there was a

concepts about the meaning of human life, our past, present and future, ourselves, others, the age of this world, our career, our goals, our family, our relationships

living transaction, a living contact. We all need a direct, personal, living contact with the living person of the Son of God.

Today many of us earnestly desire to live Christ. But to live Christ we need revelation. As we have pointed out again and again, the only way revelation can come to us is if we drop our concepts. We also need to pray, "Lord, I trust in You to defeat the god of this age. Apart from You, I do not worship anything. Lord, I turn my heart to You, and I drop all my concepts. I don't want to worship anyone other than You." If you pray in this way, the light will shine, and you will receive revelation. If you drop your concepts and turn your heart to the Lord, the veils will be taken away, and the god of this age will have no ground in your being.

The light is here, and it is shining. Our problem is that our heart is turned away to many other things, and therefore we are covered with layer upon layer of veils. This enables the god of this age to have ground in us. As a result, our thoughts are darkened, blinded, and hardened, and we cannot receive revelation, even though we may read the Bible and listen to messages. Oh, how we need revelation!

If we would see such a revelation of the living person, we must begin by dropping our veils, our concepts. Second, we need to turn our hearts to the Lord. According to 2 Corinthians 3:16, when the heart turns to the Lord, the veil will be taken away. The more you turn your heart to the Lord, the less ground the god of this age will have in your life and in your being. Then you will be under the shining of the heavenly light, and you will receive the revelation of the living person.

I can testify that in the early years of my Christian life, I had little revelation. I was veiled. But one day the veils began to drop, and the light shined into me. Since that time, the light has been coming again and again. For this reason, it is not difficult for me to receive revelation. Let us all drop the veils and, by His mercy and grace, turn our hearts to Him. (*Life-study of Galatians,* pp. 36-38)

Further Reading: Life-study of Galatians, msg. 4

Enlightenment and inspiration: We should receive light and unveiling, unloading of our natural thought every day so that daily we receive fresh light and fresh seeing of Christ and the church, His embodiment

Hymns, #538

1   It is God's intent and pleasure
     To have Christ revealed in me,
     Nothing outward as religion,
     But His Christ within to be.

     It is God's intent and pleasure
       That His Christ be wrought in me;
     Nothing outwardly performing,
     But His Christ my all to be.

2   It is God's intent and pleasure
     That His Christ may live in me;
     Nothing as an outward practise,
     But Christ working inwardly.

3   It is God's intent and pleasure
     That His Christ be formed in me;
     Not the outward forms to follow,
     But Christ growing inwardly.

4   It is God's intent and pleasure
     That His Christ make home in me;
     Not just outwardly to serve Him,
     But Christ dwelling inwardly.

5   It is God's intent and pleasure
     That His Christ my hope may be;
     It is not objective glory,
     But 'tis Christ subjectively.

6   It is God's intent and pleasure
     That His Christ be all in me;
     Nothing outwardly possessing,
     But His Christ eternally.

Composition for prophecy with main point and sub-points: _____

_____

_____

_____

_____

_____

_____

_____

_____

_____

_____

_____

_____

_____

_____

_____

_____

_____

_____

_____

_____

_____

_____

_____

_____

_____

_____

_____

_____

_____

_____

_____

_____

_____

_____

**The Way to Receive, Experience,
and Enjoy the All-inclusive Christ
as the All-inclusive Life-giving Spirit—
the Aggregate of the All-embracing
Blessing of the Full Gospel of God**

Scripture Reading: Gal. 1:15-16; 2:20; 4:19; 3:14

Day 1   I. **Galatians reveals that God's plan according to His good pleasure is to work Christ Himself into us; the most evil thing, according to Galatians, is to distract people from Christ (Eph. 1:5; Gal. 1:4-16; 2:20; 4:19; *Hymns*, #538).**

Day 2 II. **Galatians presents the Christ who is the threefold seed in humanity for God's dispensing of Himself into the believers of Christ for the fulfillment of His economy (3:16; Gen. 3:15; Gal. 4:4; Luke 8:5a, 11; John 12:24):**

   A. Christ as the seed of the woman refers to the incarnated Christ, the complete God becoming a perfect man through the dispensing of Himself into humanity in order to destroy Satan and to save the believers in Christ from sin and death (Gen. 3:15; Isa. 7:14; Matt. 1:16, 20-21, 23; Gal. 4:4; John 1:1, 14; Heb. 2:14; 1 Cor. 15:53-57).

   B. Christ as the seed of Abraham is for the blessing to all the families of the earth; the unique seed of Abraham as the last Adam became the life-giving Spirit, who is the blessing of Abraham (the reality of the good land), for the dispensing of Himself into the believers of Christ to make them the corporate seed of Abraham (Gen. 12:2-3, 7; 17:7-8; Gal. 3:14, 16, 29; John 14:17-20; 1 Cor. 15:45b; John 12:24; Isa. 53:10).

   C. Christ as the seed of David refers to the resurrected Christ, who carries out God's New Testament economy for the dispensing of the

processed Triune God into the members of His
Body, so that they may share His kingship in
His resurrection in the eternal kingdom (2 Sam.
7:12-14a; Matt. 22:42-45; Rom. 1:3; Rev. 22:16;
Acts 2:30-31; Matt. 16:16-18; Rev. 20:4, 6):

1. The great mountain, the kingdom of God
   that fills the whole earth in Daniel 2:34-35,
   is the corporate threefold seed in humanity,
   which includes all the believers in Christ
   (cf. Mark 4:26).
2. Through Christ as the threefold seed in humanity, the enemies are gone, the blessing
   is here, and we are in the kingdom; this is
   the revelation of the entire Bible.

Day 3 III. **Galatians reveals the way to receive, experience, and enjoy the all-inclusive Christ as
the all-inclusive life-giving Spirit—the aggregate of the all-embracing blessing of the
full gospel of God (3:14):**

A. The way to receive, experience, and enjoy the
all-inclusive Christ as the all-inclusive life-
giving Spirit is by God's revealing of Christ in
us; we live the Christian life according to the
Christ whom we have seen (1:16a; Eph. 1:17;
Gen. 13:14-18; Eph. 3:8, 19).

B. The way to receive, experience, and enjoy the
all-inclusive Christ as the all-inclusive life-
giving Spirit is by our receiving of Christ out of
the hearing of faith (Gal. 3:2):

1. The faith of the believers is Christ entering
   into them to be their faith, making their
   spirit a spirit of faith (Heb. 12:2a; Gal. 2:16;
   Rom. 3:22; 2 Cor. 4:13).
2. Faith comes out of the hearing of the word
   (Rom. 10:17).
3. Faith is to believe that God is and we are
   not; faith always annuls us and reveals
   Christ to us (Heb. 11:6; Gen. 5:24; John
   8:58; Gal. 2:20).

4. The believers are the members of the family, the household, of faith; this faith-house is a house that believes in God through His word (6:10).

Day 4 C. The way to receive, experience, and enjoy the all-inclusive Christ as the all-inclusive life-giving Spirit is by being born according to the Spirit and by being given the Spirit of God's Son into our hearts (4:29b, 6).

D. The way to receive, experience, and enjoy the all-inclusive Christ as the all-inclusive life-giving Spirit is by putting on Christ through the baptism that puts us into Christ (3:27).

E. The way to receive, experience, and enjoy the all-inclusive Christ as the all-inclusive life-giving Spirit is by being identified with Him in His death so that it may be no longer we who live but He who lives in us; and the life which we now live in the flesh we live by the faith of Christ (2:20):

   1. To be identified with Christ means to be one spirit with Him and even to be one entity with Him (1 Cor. 15:45b; 6:17; Phil. 1:20-21a).

   2. We are identified with Christ in His death in order that it may be no longer we who live but Christ who lives in us (Rom. 6:3-4; Gal. 2:20a).

   3. We live such a life in Christ as our faith; genuine faith is Christ Himself infused into us to become our appreciation of Him as a reaction to His attraction (v. 20b; 2 Cor. 5:14-15; Heb. 12:2a).

Day 5 F. The way to receive, experience, and enjoy the all-inclusive Christ as the all-inclusive life-giving Spirit is by living and walking by the Spirit (Gal. 5:16, 25).

G. The way to receive, experience, and enjoy the all-inclusive Christ as the all-inclusive life-giving Spirit is by having Christ formed in us through travail (4:19):

1. Christ's being formed in us depends on our being transformed; our being transformed and His being formed in us cause us to be conformed to His image (2 Cor. 3:18; Rom. 8:29).

2. To have Christ formed in us is to have the three parts of our soul (our mind, emotion, and will) renewed (12:2; 2 Cor. 4:16).

Day 6

H. The way to receive, experience, and enjoy the all-inclusive Christ as the all-inclusive life-giving Spirit is by sowing unto the Spirit with the desire and aim of the Spirit in view, to accomplish what the Spirit desires (Gal. 6:7-8).

I. The way to receive, experience, and enjoy the all-inclusive Christ as the all-inclusive life-giving Spirit is by boasting in the cross of Christ and living a new creation (vv. 14-15).

J. The way to receive, experience, and enjoy the all-inclusive Christ as the all-inclusive life-giving Spirit is by the grace of the Lord Jesus Christ with our spirit (vv. 17-18).

Morning Nourishment

Eph. Predestinating us unto sonship through Jesus Christ
1:5 to Himself, according to the good pleasure of His will.

Gal. Who gave Himself for our sins that He might rescue
1:4 us out of the present evil age according to the will of
our God and Father.

4:19 My children, with whom I travail again in birth until
Christ is formed in you.

The most evil thing, according to Galatians, is to distract people from Christ. God's will is to reveal Christ into us, to have Christ live in us, and to have Christ formed in us. This is God's purpose. Yet religion is something that distracts people from this purpose. To human eyes it does not appear so evil, but to God's eyes it is the most evil thing. God's intention is to work Christ into us, but Satan's subtlety is to use religion to keep us away from Christ. It appears good and cultured, yet religion severs more people from Christ than anything else.

To visit the casinos…is undoubtedly to be severed from Christ. But to be religious is considered as approved and commendable behavior. Yet Paul says in Galatians 5 that to be religious is to be severed from Christ, to be fallen from grace. If we have God's point of view, we will see that anything that severs people from Christ is evil. Even the most moral, ethical, and religious things are evil in the eyes of God, because they sever us from the indwelling Christ. (*The Indwelling Christ in the Canons of the New Testament*, p. 114)

Today's Reading

There could be many things in our life which take the place of the Lord Himself. My burden is to fellowship with you and help you to realize that God's plan is to work Christ Himself into you (Gal. 1:16; 2:20; 4:19). This is God's goal, His ultimate intention. Do not think God's intention is to make you merely spiritual. Even spirituality might become something in you that is in contradiction to God's plan. The work for the Lord, the activities in Christianity, the progress for the gospel, and so many other good things could possibly be a hindrance, a substitute for Christ.

I knew some sisters who loved to fellowship with other sisters. This kind of fellowship eventually became a hindrance between them and the Lord and took the place of the Lord in their lives. They loved this kind of fellowship more than Christ Himself. With these sisters there was the need to be converted, not from anything sinful but from this good fellowship to Christ Himself....Regeneration is a conversion, but a conversion to us Christians is not just once for all. We need many conversions. Anything, no matter how good it might be, can become a hindrance, a barrier between you and Christ, taking the place of Christ in your life and substituting Christ in your life. May we all be converted from everything other than Christ to the living person of Christ Himself.

We must remember that God's plan is to work Christ into us, and we have to pay attention to Christ Himself, nothing else. We do not agree that anything would come into our life to take the place of Christ. We like to count everything as a loss on account of the excellency of the knowledge of Christ Jesus our Lord. Paul's desire was "to know Him and the power of His resurrection and the fellowship of His sufferings, being conformed to His death" (Phil. 3:10). Paul wanted to be mingled with Christ, to be transformed into Christ in order to become a real member of Christ. If you would seek and experience Christ in this way, you will have the power, the fruit, the spirituality, and everything which is good in the eyes of God. The reason for this is that everything which is good in the eyes of God must be something of Christ Himself. If you have Christ, you will have everything.

God's plan is to work Christ into us, so throughout our life we need many conversions. Whenever there is something in your life substituting Christ, you need a conversion from that very thing to Christ Himself. We should always keep ourselves in direct contact with Christ. Then we will be one with Christ in reality. (*A Young Man in God's Plan,* pp. 28-32)

Further Reading: The Indwelling Christ in the Canons of the New Testament, chs. 11-12; A Young Man in God's Plan, ch. 3

Enlightenment and inspiration: _____

_____

_____

_____

Morning Nourishment

Gen. And I will put enmity between you and the woman
3:15 and between your seed and her seed; he will bruise
       you on the head, but you will bruise him on the heel.
Gal. But to Abraham were the promises spoken and to
3:16 his seed. He does not say, "And to the seeds," as con-
       cerning many, but as concerning one: "And to your
       seed," who is Christ.
4:4   But when the fullness of the time came, God sent
       forth His Son, born of a woman, born under law.

Christ as the seed of the woman, the seed of Abraham, and the
seed of David is a threefold seed and also a threefold dispensing.
God promised that the seed of the woman would bruise the head
of the serpent. This is the first aspect of God's dispensing.

God's promise to Abraham that his seed would be the blessing
to all the nations was the second aspect of His dispensing. This
blessing to all the nations is the Spirit. The seed of Abraham is
Christ as the last Adam (1 Cor. 15:45b). This last Adam, the
God-man, eventually became the life-giving Spirit. A man who
was the seed of Abraham became a Spirit, even a life-giving Spirit
(1 Cor. 15:45b). John 1:14 reveals that the Word became flesh.
Then, according to 1 Corinthians 15:45, Christ as the last Adam
became a life-giving Spirit....In order to impart God into man, the
man Jesus had to die and be resurrected so that He could become
a life-giving Spirit. How marvelous this is!

Christ as the seed of David was begotten through His resurrection to be the firstborn Son of God and God's sure mercies
shown to David (Acts 13:33-34). This is the third aspect of His dispensing. (*The Central Line of the Divine Revelation*, pp. 93-94)

to continue producing kings to reign in God's kingdom which began with David

Today's Reading

The divine economy and the divine dispensing in the promises
of the seed of the woman, the seed of Abraham, and the seed of
David have a threefold purpose: first, to destroy Satan and to save
us from sin and death; second, to cause us to inherit the

consummated Triune God as our blessing and inheritance; and third, to cause us to share Christ's kingship. These three items cover God's full salvation in a complete way. God's full salvation is to deliver us out of the hand of Satan and out of sin and death, to bring us into the full inheritance of God Himself as our blessing, and to cause us to share the kingship with Christ as His co-kings in the kingdom age.

Nearly every page of the sixty-six books of the Bible is occupied with the threefold seed in humanity. This threefold seed in humanity is God who became a man. First, He became the seed of the woman to overcome all the enemies—Satan, sin, death, and man's self. Second, He became the seed of Abraham to be the consummated Triune God. This consummation began with incarnation and ended in resurrection. In resurrection this incarnated One became the life-giving Spirit (1 Cor. 15:45b). This is a great truth in the Bible.

The conclusion of my study of the Bible is that the Triune God, the complete, eternal God, one day became a threefold seed in humanity, first, to destroy God's enemies, second, to cause Himself to be consummated for the blessing of His chosen people, and third, to be the seed of David to bring in the kingdom. He came not just to be a blessing to His chosen people but to set His chosen people up as a kingdom. This kingdom is the great mountain in Daniel 2:34-35 that will fill the whole earth. The great mountain is the corporate threefold seed in humanity, which includes all the believers in Christ. We are all incorporated in that great mountain.

The threefold seed in humanity first dealt with all the enemies; second, He became the consummated Triune God as our full blessing, intensified sevenfold; and third, He made His chosen people His kingdom that fills not only the earth but also the heavens, causing the whole universe to become His great kingdom. The enemies are gone, the blessing is here, and we are in the kingdom. This is the revelation of the entire Bible. How wonderful this is! (*The Central Line of the Divine Revelation,* pp. 90, 149-150)

Further Reading: The Central Line of the Divine Revelation, msgs. 8-9, 13

Enlightenment and inspiration: _____

_____

_____

_____

Morning Nourishment

Gal. This only I wish to learn from you, Did you receive
3:2 the Spirit out of the works of law or out of the hear-
      ing of faith?

Rom. So faith *comes* out of hearing, and hearing through
10:17 the word of Christ.

Heb. But without faith it is impossible to be well pleasing
11:6 *to Him,* for he who comes forward to God must be-
      lieve that He is and that He is a rewarder of those
      who diligently seek Him.

The faith of the believers is actually not their own faith but Christ entering into them to be their faith (Rom. 3:22 and note 1; Gal. 2:16 and note 1). Now we need to consider how and when Christ entered into us to be our faith. When we repented unto God, the pneumatic Christ as the sanctifying Spirit of God (1 Pet. 1:2a) moved within us to be our faith by which we believed on the Lord Jesus (Acts 16:31). Romans 10:17 says, "So faith comes out of hearing, and hearing through the word of Christ." As sinners we did not have faith. Faith came into us by our hearing the word. This word is just Christ Himself.

The preachers preach Christ to present Christ's beauty. After hearing such a word about Christ, that is, after seeing such a Christ, within you there is an appreciation of Christ, and your ap-preciation of Him is the reaction to His attraction. We can believe in the Lord Jesus because we hear about Him, that is, we see Him. We read the Bible, and in the Bible we see something about Him. (*Crystallization-study of the Epistle to the Romans,* pp. 69-70)

Today's Reading

When the proper preaching of the gospel is going on, the Spirit, the pneumatic Christ, accompanies that preaching. That preach-ing speaks Christ outside of you, but the pneumatic Christ right away accompanies that preaching and works within you. Then you repent and appreciate such a One. Spontaneously something within you rises up. This is your faith, your believing. Your believ-ing comes from your knowing of Christ. Your believing actually is your appreciation of Christ as a reaction to His attraction. Only the believers, not the sinners, have this kind of reaction.

If you see this point, you will say, "Lord Jesus, even my believing in You is You Yourself. You are so attractive and beauteous! Who can help but believe in You?" Many young people have been attracted by the Savior's beauty. Even if their parents persecute them and threaten them to death, they will not give up their faith in Christ. This kind of faith is Christ Himself. By such a faith the believing ones believe that God raised Jesus Christ from the dead that they may be saved (Rom. 10:9b-10a; 5:1). They have access through faith into the grace in which they now stand (Rom. 5:2).

He who comes forward to God must believe that God is (Heb. 11:6b). This is very simple. God requires you only to believe that He is. The verb *to be* is actually the divine title of our Triune God. In Exodus 3 Moses asked God what His name was. God answered that His name is I AM WHO I AM (vv. 13-14). Our God's name is the verb *to be*. He is "I AM WHO I AM." He is the only One.

This means that in the whole universe, nothing else is. Only One is. He is, because He is real. All other things created by Him are not real. This is why Solomon, the wise king, said that all things are vanity (Eccl. 1:2). You think you are, but you are vanity....Faith is to stop you from doing anything but to make God everything to you. This equals Paul's word in Galatians 2:20: "I am crucified with Christ; and it is no longer I who live, but it is Christ who lives in me." Who lives? It is no longer I. I do not exist. I was terminated. I was crucified. I am finished. It is no more I, but Christ lives in me. Christ lives. Christ is. Christ exists. I do not exist. This is the very essence of the short word *believe that God is*. To believe that God is implies that you are not. He must be the only One, the unique One, in everything, and we must be nothing in everything. (*Crystallization-study of the Epistle to the Romans*, pp. 70-71, 73-75)

Further Reading: Crystallization-study of the Epistle to the Romans, msgs. 7-10; *The Central Line of the Divine Revelation,* msg. 13

Enlightenment and inspiration: _____

_____

_____

_____

Morning Nourishment

Gal. I am crucified with Christ; and *it is* no longer I *who*
2:20 live, but *it is* Christ *who* lives in me; and the *life* which I
now live in the flesh I live in faith, the *faith* of the Son
of God, who loved me and gave Himself up for me.

3:14 In order that the blessing of Abraham might come to
the Gentiles in Christ Jesus, that we might receive
the promise of the Spirit through faith.

Rom. Or are you ignorant that all of us who have been bap-
6:3-4 tized into Christ Jesus have been baptized into His
death? We have been buried therefore with Him
through baptism into His death, in order that just as
Christ was raised from the dead through the glory of
the Father, so also we might walk in newness of life.

[One] way in Galatians to experience the all-inclusive Christ
as the life-giving Spirit is by being identified with Him so that it
may be no longer we who live but He who lives in us; and the life
which we now live in the flesh we live in the faith of Christ (Gal.
2:20). To be identified with Christ is to be made one with Christ.
Baptism identifies us with Christ by making us one entity with
Christ. We are identified with Christ especially in His death. [Ac-
cording to Romans 6:3]...we have been baptized into two things—
into Christ and into His death. Therefore, we are now one entity
with Christ in His death. This means that He died, and we died
also. His death is our death. With Him, His death is history, but
with us, it is a present, living, vivid experience. When we are baptized, we are put into Christ's death, making Christ's death ours.
Since we are dead and buried, how could we live any longer? We
have been identified with Christ in His death that it may be no
longer we who live but He who lives in us; and the life which we
now live in the flesh we live in the faith of Christ. (*The Central
Line of the Divine Revelation,* pp. 156-157)

Today's Reading

To live in the faith of Christ means that the very Christ who
lives in us becomes our faith. Galatians 2:20 says that it is no

longer we who live, but it is Christ who lives in us. It then goes on to say that the life that we now live, we still live in the flesh, yet we live this life by Christ as our faith. Christ is living within us, and this living Christ within us eventually becomes our faith. It is by this faith, which is the very realization of Christ, that we still live in the flesh. This kind of living is actually not we who live but Christ who lives in us;...we still live in the flesh by Christ as our faith. Thus, the life spoken of in Galatians 2:20 is a life that is absolutely Christ.

Christ's living in us must be a fact, not merely a doctrine or a declaration. When we awake in the morning, we should call on the Lord a number of times before we do anything else. If we will do this, by the time we have made our beds, we will be different persons. Calling on the Lord in this way will help us to experience Christ living in us. Copying two verses from the Bible after our morning revival and taking them in a little at a time throughout the day will also help us to experience Christ living in us. We should not care merely for the doctrine of Christ living in us. We should care for the fact.

According to Galatians 2:20, the life which we now live in the flesh we live in the faith of Christ. We live a life in the flesh, but we live this life in the faith of Christ. We do not live such a life in our faith but in Christ's faith, even in Christ as our faith.

We all need to see that our believing in Jesus and our being baptized into Him means that He comes into us and we are put into Him so that He and we become one. He is in us, and we are in Him. This is possible only because of the two spirits. He is the divine Spirit, and we have a human spirit. The divine Spirit is in our human spirit. Therefore, in our spirit we are one spirit with Him. He died, and we died in Him. We live, but He lives in us. We are still living, yet we live this life not by anything of ourselves but by Him as everything, even as our faith. We all need to see this. This is not merely a doctrine; it must be our experience. (*The Central Line of the Divine Revelation,* pp. 157, 162-163)

Further Reading: The Central Line of the Divine Revelation, msgs. 13-14

Enlightenment and inspiration: _____

_____

_____

_____

Morning Nourishment

Gal. My children, with whom I travail again in birth un-
4:19 til Christ is formed in you.
5:16 But I say, Walk by the Spirit and you shall by no
      means fulfill the lust of the flesh.
25 If we live by the Spirit, let us also walk by the Spirit.
Rom. And do not be fashioned according to this age, but
12:2 be transformed by the renewing of the mind...

[Another] way to receive, experience, and enjoy the all-
inclusive Christ as the all-inclusive life-giving Spirit is by
living and walking by the Spirit (Gal. 5:16, 25). Living and
walking by the Spirit is equivalent to having our being by the
Spirit. The Spirit is in our human spirit (Rom. 8:16). It is often
difficult in Paul's writings for translators to determine
whether *spirit* should be capitalized or not. The spirit in Paul's
writings is the mingled spirit, the Spirit who is in our spirit.
      After rising up in the morning, we should do everything by
our spirit. We must begin our day by living and walking in our
spirit. If we rise up in a loose way, we will spoil the whole day.
The best thing to do after rising up is to call on the name of the
Lord. When we call "O Lord Jesus," we are in the spirit (1 Cor.
12:3). Calling in this way brings us back from everything to
our spirit. Then we will have a good beginning of the day, and
we will be able to face any situation. We will be able to encoun-
ter every circumstance by our spirit. This is to live and to walk
by the Spirit. This experience follows the experience of being
identified with Christ in His death in order that He may live
in us. Without experiencing the identification with Christ, we
cannot live and walk by the Spirit. (*The Central Line of the Divine Revelation,* p. 163)

Today's Reading

The way to receive, experience, and enjoy Christ as the
Spirit is also by having Christ formed in us through travail
[Gal. 4:19]....In Galatians 1:16 Christ is revealed in us; in 2:20
Christ lives in us; and in 3:27 Christ is upon us, clothing us

like a garment. Now, in 4:19 Christ is formed in us.

[In Romans 12:2a] the term *renewing* is used with *transformed*. This indicates that to have Christ formed in us is to have the three parts of our soul—our mind, emotion, and will—renewed. Our mind is the leading part of our soul. To have our mind renewed is to have Christ "invade" our mind. Our mind, emotion, and will are filled with our self and the world. To be renewed in our mind is to remove our self and the world from our mind, emotion, and will and replace them with Christ. If we are renewed in this way, Christ will be formed in us, and our mind, emotion, and will will be like Him. Every part of our inner being will bear the image of Christ. This is to have Christ formed in us. When we think, we will be like Christ. When we love or hate, like or dislike, we will be like Christ. When we choose or reject, we will be like Christ.

However, most of us are not like this yet. At times we may think noble thoughts, but in our practical life our mind is not like Christ. Our mind simply expresses our self with the world. It is the same with our emotion. We may love, laugh, and weep by the self and the world, not by Christ. This indicates that Christ has not been formed in us. Christ has not invaded our mind, emotion, and will to replace the self and the world with Himself. Many times when people talk, their talk is full of the self and the element of the world. The mind, emotion, and will of such persons are filled with the self and the element of the world. What is formed in them is the self with the world, and they are the expression of the self and the world. We can never be an expression of Christ until Christ has invaded our entire inner being to chase the self and the world out of our mind, emotion, and will and replace them with Himself. Then our inner being will bear the form, the image, of Christ. (*The Central Line of the Divine Revelation,* pp. 163-165)

Further Reading: The Central Line of the Divine Revelation, msg. 14

Enlightenment and inspiration: _____

_____

_____

Morning Nourishment

Gal. ...He who sows unto the Spirit will of the Spirit
6:8 reap eternal life.

14-15 But far be it from me to boast except in the cross of
our Lord Jesus Christ, through whom the world has
been crucified to me and I to the world. For neither
is circumcision anything nor uncircumcision, but a
new creation *is what matters.*

18 The grace of our Lord Jesus Christ be with your
spirit, brothers. Amen.

The way to receive, experience, and enjoy Christ as the
Spirit is also by boasting in the cross of Christ and living a
new creation, which is neither religion nor nonreligion (Gal.
6:14-15). The cross of Christ is our boast. We boast in the fact
that everything has been terminated on the cross. The love of
cars, the love of a big house, and the love of stylish fashions
have all been terminated. Everything has been "crossed out."
This is our boast. Now we are living a new creation. Since we
boast in the cross, we cannot live in the old creation; we must
live in the new creation. Everything must be new because we
are a new creation in Christ. This is the way to enjoy Christ.
(*The Central Line of the Divine Revelation,* p. 167)

Today's Reading

Another way to receive, experience, and enjoy the all-inclusive
Christ as the all-inclusive life-giving Spirit is by sowing unto
the Spirit with the desire and aim of the Spirit in view, to accomplish what the Spirit desires (Gal. 6:7, 8b). Our human
living is a sowing. Whatever we do, we are sowing seeds, and
whatever we sow, we will reap. If we sow something high and
good, we will reap the same, and if we sow something mean
and low, we can expect to reap the same thing. Everything
that we do in our daily life is a sowing. We should not think
that the way we comb our hair is a small matter. Even this is a
sowing. After a certain period of time, we will reap what we

have sown [Gal. 6:8]....We must endeavor to sow properly. If we sow according to the Spirit, we will reap according to the Spirit.

Our sowing unto the Spirit is with the desire and aim of the Spirit in view. Our desire and aim are not ours but the Spirit's. Christ lives in us, but our sowing may be according to our own desire....In our sowing we must have the desire and aim of the Spirit in view, to accomplish the aim of the Spirit. Whatever we have, wear, or do should correspond with the Spirit's purpose, desire, and intention. What we will reap depends on what we sow.

To sow to the Spirit in this way is to receive, experience, and enjoy the Spirit as the all-embracing blessing of the gospel. If we live a life without the Spirit and sow according to the flesh, we cannot expect to enjoy Christ as the all-embracing blessing....There are many millions of Christians in America today, but how many of them are living Christ? How many are living Christ in the way that they comb their hair or purchase shoes? This is not a small matter. Our purchasing of a necktie is a sowing. The reaping will come when we stand before people with our tie to preach the gospel. If the tie is too worldly, our preaching will be empty. If we are not dressed according to the Spirit, people will not have the heart to listen to our message. To sow to the Spirit is to live Christ, and this is to receive, experience, and enjoy Christ.

The consummate way to receive, experience, and enjoy Christ as the Spirit is by the grace of the Lord Jesus Christ with our spirit. The book of Galatians concludes with 6:18: "The grace of our Lord Jesus Christ be with your spirit, brothers. Amen." The grace of the Lord Jesus Christ being with our Spirit is the way to receive, experience, and enjoy Christ. (*The Central Line of the Divine Revelation*, pp. 166-168)

Further Reading: The Central Line of the Divine Revelation, msg. 14

Enlightenment and inspiration: _____
_____
_____
_____

Hymns, #499

1   Oh, what a life! Oh, what a peace!
    The Christ who's all within me lives.
    With Him I have been crucified;
    This glorious fact to me He gives.
    Now it's no longer I that live,
    But Christ the Lord within me lives.

2   Oh, what a joy! Oh, what a rest!
    Christ now is being formed in me.
    His very nature and life divine
    In my whole being inwrought shall be.
    All that I am came to an end,
    And all of Christ is all to me.

3   Oh, what a thought! Oh, what a boast!
    Christ shall in me be magnified.
    In nothing shall I be ashamed,
    For He in all shall be applied.
    In woe or blessing, death or life,
    Through me shall Christ be testified.

4   Oh, what a prize! Oh, what a gain!
    Christ is the goal toward which I press.
    Nothing I treasure, nor aught desire,
    But Christ of all-inclusiveness.
    My hope, my glory, and my crown
    Is Christ, the One of peerlessness.

(Repeat the last two lines of each stanza)

Composition for prophecy with main point and sub-points: _____

_____

_____

_____

_____

_____

_____

_____

_____

_____

_____

_____

_____

_____

_____

_____

_____

_____

_____

_____

_____

_____

_____

_____

_____

_____

_____

_____

_____

_____

_____

_____

Paul's Gospel

Scripture Reading: Gal. 1:6-12, 15-16, 23; 2:2, 4-5, 7, 14, 16; 3:8, 14

Day 1   I. **The purpose of the book of Galatians is to cause its recipients to know that the gospel preached by the apostle Paul was not from man's teaching but from God's revelation (1:11-12):**

A. Paul desired to rescue the churches in Galatia, which had been distracted by Judaism with its law, and to bring them back to the grace of the gospel (vv. 6-12; 5:4).

B. The law dealt with man in the old creation, whereas the gospel makes man a new creation in resurrection (1:1, 6-12; 2:20; 6:15).

Day 2 II. **The gospel is the fulfillment of the entire Old Testament (Mark 1:1, 14):**

A. The gospel is the fulfillment of the promises, prophecies, and types and is also the removal of the law; this is a full definition of the gospel (Gen. 3:15, 21).

B. The gospel preached to Abraham was the unveiling of God's heart; the promise God gave to Abraham was the gospel (12:3; 22:17-18; Gal. 3:6-14).

C. Christ, the unique One, is the fulfillment of the entire Old Testament; this means that the fulfillment of the promises, prophecies, and types and the removal of the law are a living person, Jesus Christ (Matt. 17:2-8; Rom. 10:4).

D. The gospel is the fulfillment of the great promise concerning the seed of the woman for the destruction of the serpent and of the great promise concerning the seed of Abraham for bringing in the blessing of the Spirit, who is the consummation of the Triune God as eternal life to be our blessing (Gen. 3:15; 22:17-18; Heb. 2:14; John 3:14; Gal. 3:14).

Day 3 III. **Galatians affords us a complete revelation of the truth, the reality, of the gospel, not in detail but in certain basic principles (2:5, 14):**

A. The first aspect of the truth of the gospel is that fallen man cannot be justified out of works of law (v. 16a).

B. Under God's New Testament economy, we are not to keep the law; rather, we are justified out of faith in Christ (v. 16b):

1. Through believing we are joined to Christ and become one with Him (John 3:15).

2. Faith in Christ denotes an organic union with Him through believing; the term *in Christ* refers to this organic union (Gal. 2:17; 3:14, 28; 5:6).

3. Justification is not merely a matter of position; it is also an organic matter, a matter in life.

4. It is by means of our organic union with Christ that God can reckon Christ as our righteousness; only in this way can we be justified by God (1 Cor. 1:30).

Day 4 C. In God's New Testament economy, we have life and live by faith (Gal. 3:11).

D. We are dead to the law, we are alive to God, and we have Christ living in us (2:19-20).

E. In Christ we are a new creation (6:15).

Day 5 IV. **Paul's gospel is the unique gospel, the complete gospel (1:7; Col. 1:25):**

A. Paul's gospel includes all the aspects of the gospel in the four Gospels:

1. In Matthew the goal of the gospel of the kingdom is to bring people into God to make them citizens of the kingdom of the heavens (28:19; 24:14; Rom. 14:17; Gal. 5:21).

2. In Mark the preaching of the gospel is to

bring part of the old creation into the new creation (16:15-16; Rom. 8:20-21; Gal. 6:15).

3. In Luke we have the gospel of forgiveness to bring redeemed people back to the God-ordained blessing (24:46-48; 1:77-79; 2:30-32; Eph. 1:3, 7; Gal. 3:14).

4. In John we have the eternal life that we may bear fruit for the building up of the Body of Christ, which is Christ's increase (20:31; 15:16; Rom. 8:10, 6, 11; 12:4-5; Gal. 3:28; 4:19; 6:10, 16).

B. Paul's gospel is the center of the New Testament revelation (Rom. 1:1, 9):

1. Paul's gospel is a revelation of the Triune God processed to become the all-inclusive life-giving Spirit (1 Cor. 15:45b; 2 Cor. 3:17; Gal. 3:2, 5, 14).

2. Paul's gospel is centered on the Triune God being our life in order to be one with us and to make us one with Him, that we may be the Body of Christ to express Christ in a corporate way (Rom. 8:11; 12:4-5; Eph. 1:22-23).

Day 6 V. **Christ, a living person, is the focus of Paul's gospel; hence, the book of Galatians is emphatically Christ-centered (1:15-16):**

A. Christ was crucified to redeem us out of the curse of the law and rescue us out of the evil religious course of the world (3:1, 13; 1:4, 15-16).

B. Christ was resurrected from the dead that He might live in us (v. 1; 2:20).

C. We were baptized into Christ, being identified with Him, and we have put on Christ, clothing ourselves with Him; thus, we are in Christ and have become of Him (3:27-29; 5:24).

D. Christ has been revealed in us, He is now living in us, and He will be formed in us (1:16; 2:20; 4:19).

E. To Christ the law has conducted us, and in Christ we are all sons of God (3:24, 26).

F. In Christ we inherit God's promised blessing and enjoy the all-inclusive Spirit (v. 14).

G. In Christ we all are one (v. 28).

H. We should not be deprived of all profit from Christ and thus be separated, severed, from Him (5:4).

I. We need Christ to supply us with grace in our spirit that we may live Him (6:18).

J. God's desire is that His chosen people receive His Son into them; this is the gospel (1:15-16; 2:20; 4:19).

VI. **The focal point of Paul's gospel is God Himself in His Trinity becoming the processed all-inclusive Spirit to be life and everything to us for our enjoyment so that He and we may be one to express Him for eternity (vv. 4, 6; 3:13-14, 26-28; 6:15).**

Morning Nourishment

Mark The beginning of the gospel of Jesus Christ, the
1:1   Son of God.
Gen. And I will put enmity between you and the woman
3:15 and between your seed and her seed; he will bruise
      you on the head, but you will bruise him on the heel.
Heb. Since therefore the children have shared in blood
2:14 and flesh, He also Himself in like manner partook
      of the same, that through death He might destroy
      him who has the might of death, that is, the devil.
Gal. In order that the blessing of Abraham might come
3:14 to the Gentiles in Christ Jesus, that we might re-
      ceive the promise of the Spirit through faith.

The gospel is the fulfillment of the Old Testament. Now we
need to ask what the contents of the Old Testament are. We
may use three words to express the contents of the Old Testament: promise, law, and prophecy.

The gospel is the fulfillment of the promises, prophecies,
and types in the Old Testament and the removal of the law.
Both the fulfillment of the promises, prophecies, and types
and the removal of the law are a living person, Jesus Christ.
Christ Himself is the fulfillment, and He Himself is the removal of the law....The beginning of the gospel is actually the
ushering in of this living person. For us today, Christ is everything. As long as we have Him, we have everything. We do not
have promises—we have Christ. We do not have prophecies—
we have Christ. We do not have types—we have Christ. We do
not strive to keep the law, because Christ is here, and we have
Him. In our spiritual dictionary the unique word is Christ.
(*Life-study of Mark,* pp. 22-23, 41-42)

Today's Reading

The first promise [given by God] is recorded in Genesis
3:15....This promise was given immediately after the fall of
man. Probably Adam and Eve were in fear and trembling

because of their disobedience. But God gave them a marvelous promise. This promise was that a seed of the woman would come to bruise the head of the serpent. Although his heel would be bruised, the seed of woman would nevertheless crush the serpent's head. What a great promise this is! The gospel is the fulfillment of the promise that the seed of the woman would crush the head of the serpent. We know that Christ, the seed of woman, did come. He was born of a virgin as the fulfillment of the promise in Genesis 3:15.

Another promise, also concerning the seed, was given to Abraham [Gen. 22:17-18; Gal. 3:16]....Abraham's seed would be a great blessing to all mankind, for all nations would be blessed through his seed.

Whereas the seed of woman is for the destruction of the serpent [Heb. 2:14], the seed of Abraham is for the blessing of God to be brought to us. The seed of woman terminates the serpent, and the seed of Abraham brings in the blessing of the Triune God. In Galatians 3:14 Paul speaks regarding this blessing....According to this verse, the blessing is the Spirit. What is this Spirit? The Spirit is the consummation of the Triune God. When we receive the Spirit, we receive the Triune God and have Him as our blessing. Furthermore, this blessing is our eternal life. The Spirit equals the Triune God, the Triune God is eternal life, and eternal life is the blessing we receive.

Now we can see more fully what the gospel is. The gospel is the fulfillment of two great promises: the promise concerning the seed of woman for the destruction of the serpent and the promise concerning the seed of Abraham for bringing in the blessing of the Spirit, who is the consummation of the Triune God as eternal life to be our blessing. (*Life-study of Mark*, pp. 22-25)

Further Reading: Life-study of Mark, msgs. 3-5; Life-study of Galatians, msg. 17

Enlightenment and inspiration: _____

_____

_____

_____

Morning Nourishment

Matt. And Peter answered and said to Jesus, Lord, it is
17:4-5 good for us to be here; if You are willing, I will
make three tents here, one for You and one for Moses and one for Elijah. While he was still speaking,
behold, a bright cloud overshadowed them, and
behold, a voice out of the cloud, saying, This is My
Son, the Beloved, in whom I have found My delight. Hear Him!

8 And when they lifted up their eyes, they saw no
one except Jesus Himself alone.

Rom. For Christ is the end of the law unto righteousness
10:4 to everyone who believes.

The gospel is the fulfillment of the promises and the prophecies and also the removal of the custody of the law. This means
that the gospel is the fulfillment of the promises and prophecies concerning the unique seed, the seed of woman and the
seed of Abraham. Furthermore, the gospel cancels, annuls, and
removes the custody of the law. Now we are no longer depend-
ent on the Old Testament promises, the law, and the prophecies, for Christ, the unique seed, has come. This seed is the
fulfillment of all the precious promises. Because we have Him,
all the promises are fulfilled. As the fulfillment of the promises,
He is also the fulfillment of the prophecies, which were given to
confirm the promises. Furthermore, with Him is the removal of
the custody of the law. Therefore, the unique seed is the fulfillment of the promises and the prophecies and the removal of the
custody of the law. (*Life-study of Mark*, p. 26)

Today's Reading

The coming of Christ was the fulfillment of the promises
and prophecies and the cancellation of the law. The law has
been removed, and God's chosen people no longer are under its
custody....The law may be compared to a sheepfold, a place
where sheep are kept at night. When day dawns, the sheep

may come out of the fold. Likewise, because Christ has come as the fulfillment of the promises and prophecies, it is no longer necessary for God's chosen people to be under the custody of the law. In a positive sense the law was a custodian, but in a negative sense the law was a bondage, a slavery. But now the law, along with the promises and the prophecies, is over. The seed of woman has destroyed the serpent, and the seed of Abraham has brought in the blessing of the Triune God. Furthermore, this One has removed the law. Now we are no longer in the dispensation of the law, the promises, or the prophecies, for we have Christ.

If we see this, we can understand the significance of what took place on the Mount of Transfiguration when Peter proposed that three tabernacles be made—one for Moses, one for Elijah, and one for the Lord Jesus. This suggestion was offensive to the heavens. Therefore, Matthew 17:5 says, "While he was still speaking, behold, a bright cloud overshadowed them, and behold, a voice out of the cloud, saying, This is My Son, the Beloved, in whom I have found My delight. Hear Him!" Then Matthew 17:8 goes on to say, "And when they lifted up their eyes, they saw no one except Jesus Himself alone." Moses represented the law, and Elijah represented the prophets. Christ, the unique One, is everything. He is the fulfillment of the promises and the prophecies and also the removal of the law. This means that He is the full replacement of the entire Old Testament. This is the gospel, the good news, the glad tidings. Praise the Lord for the gospel! Praise Him that Christ is the fulfillment of the promises and the prophecies and also the removal of the law!

The gospel is also the fulfillment of something else—the fulfillment of the types in the Old Testament. Therefore, in the gospel we have the fulfillment of the promises, the prophecies, and types. (*Life-study of Mark,* pp. 26-28)

Further Reading: Life-study of Mark, msgs. 3-5; *The Advance of the Lord's Recovery Today,* msg. 2

Enlightenment and inspiration: _____

_____

_____

_____

Morning Nourishment

Gal. 2:5   To them we yielded with the subjection *demanded* not even for an hour, that the truth of the gospel might remain with you.

    16   And knowing that a man is not justified out of works of law, but through faith in Jesus Christ, we also have believed into Christ Jesus that we might be justified out of faith in Christ and not out of the works of law, because out of the works of law no flesh will be justified.

    5:6   For in Christ Jesus neither circumcision avails anything nor uncircumcision, but faith *avails*, operating through love.

In Galatians 2:5 and 14 Paul speaks of the truth of the gospel. The word truth in these verses does not mean the doctrine or teaching of the gospel; it denotes the reality of the gospel. Although Galatians is a short book, it affords us a complete revelation of the reality of the gospel. This revelation, however, is given not in detail, but in certain basic principles. Therefore, in this message we shall cover the truth of the gospel revealed in these basic principles.

The first aspect of the truth of the gospel is that fallen man cannot be justified out of works of law. In 2:16 Paul says, "Knowing that a man is not justified out of works of law." At the end of this verse Paul declares, "Out of the works of law no flesh will be justified." The word *flesh* in 2:16 means fallen man who has become flesh (Gen. 6:3). No such man will be justified by works of law. Furthermore, in 3:11 Paul goes on to say, "That by law no one is justified before God is evident." In these verses Paul tells us clearly that no one is justified by works of law. (*Life-study of Galatians*, p. 69)

Today's Reading

The Seventh-Day Adventists insist on strict observance of the Sabbath. However, they seem to forget that by endeavoring to keep the law with respect to the Sabbath, they make themselves debtors to keep all the commandments. The New Testament says that if we keep all the commandments except one, we transgress the whole law (James 2:10). Romans 7 proves that we cannot keep all the commandments....It is impossible for fallen man to keep all of God's commandments. How ridiculous it is to go back to the law and try to keep it! We simply do not have the ability to keep the law. As Paul says in Romans 7:14, the law is spiritual, but we are fleshy, sold under sin. Therefore, by works of law shall no flesh be justified.

Under God's New Testament economy, we are not to keep the law. On the contrary, we are justified by faith in Christ (Gal. 2:16). We may be so familiar with the expression "justified out of faith in Christ" that we take it for granted. But what actually is faith in Christ, and what does it mean to be justified out of faith in Christ? Faith in Christ denotes an organic union through believing. The proper preaching of the gospel is not the preaching of a doctrine; it is the preaching of the person of the Son of God. The Son of God is the embodiment of the Father and is realized as the Spirit. To preach the gospel is to preach this person. Whenever we preach the gospel, we must impress those who hear us with the living person of the Son of God. No matter what the subject of our gospel message may be, the focal point of our preaching must be this living person.

This faith creates an organic union in which we and Christ are one. Therefore, the expression *out of faith in Christ* actually denotes an organic union accomplished by believing in Christ. The term *in Christ* refers to this organic union. Before we believed in Christ, there was a great separation between us and Christ. We were we, and Christ was Christ. But through believing we were joined to Christ and became one with Him. Now we are in Christ, and Christ is in us. This is an organic union, a union in life.... Because we and Christ are one, whatever belongs to Him is ours. This is the basis upon which God counts Christ as our righteousness. (*Life-study of Galatians,* pp. 69-70, 72, 74)

Further Reading: Life-study of Galatians, msgs. 8, 19

Enlightenment and inspiration: _____

_____
_____
_____

Morning Nourishment

Gal. And that by law no one is justified before God is ev-
3:11 ident because, "The righteous one shall have life
and live by faith."
2:19-20 For I through law have died to law that I might live
to God. I am crucified with Christ; and *it is* no longer I *who* live, but *it is* Christ *who* lives in me; and
the *life* which I now live in the flesh I live in faith,
the *faith* of the Son of God, who loved me and gave
Himself up for me.

It is by means of our organic union with Christ that God can
reckon Christ as our righteousness....Marriage is a helpful illustration of this, although it is inadequate. Suppose a poor woman is
united in marriage to a wealthy man. Through this union she
participates in the wealth of her husband. In like manner,
through our organic union with Christ, we share whatever Christ
is and has. As soon as this union takes place, in the eyes of God
Christ becomes us, and we become one with Him. Only in this
way can we be justified before God.

Many Christians have a mere doctrinal understanding of justification by faith. According to their concept, Christ is the just
One, the righteous One on the throne in the presence of God.
When we believe in Christ, God reckons Christ to be our righteousness. This understanding of justification is very shallow. As
we have pointed out, in order to be justified by faith in Christ, we
need to believe in the Lord Jesus out of an appreciation of His preciousness. As Christ's preciousness is infused into us through the
preaching of the gospel, we spontaneously appreciate the Lord
and call on Him. This is genuine believing. Through such a believing we and Christ become one. Therefore, God must reckon Him
as our righteousness. (*Life-study of Galatians*, pp. 74-75)

Today's Reading

When we believed in the Lord Jesus, we had this kind of experience, although we did not have the terminology to explain it.

When we heard the gospel, we began to sense the Lord's preciousness. This gave rise to the living faith that joined us to Christ organically. From that time onward, Christ and we became one in life and in reality. Therefore, justification by faith is not merely a matter of position. It is also an organic matter, a matter in life. The organic union with Christ is accomplished spontaneously through the living faith produced by our appreciation of Him. This is to be justified by faith in Christ.

In God's New Testament economy, man also has life by faith and lives by faith. In 3:11 Paul says, "The righteous one shall have life and live by faith."...As a result of the organic union, we have life in us. Furthermore, we live by the faith which is our appreciation of the precious Lord Jesus. We not only have life, but we also live by this life.

In 2:19 Paul says, "For I through law have died to law that I might live to God." It is very difficult to explain in doctrine what it means to die to the law so that we might live to God. It is most helpful to consider this matter in the light of our experience. Our Christian experience proves that as soon as our organic union with Christ took place, we had the sense that we were dead to the world, to sin, to the self, and to all the obligations of the law. At the same time, we were conscious of the fact that we were alive to God. Probably when we first realized this, we had neither the knowledge nor the terminology to explain it. Perhaps you said, "Lord Jesus, from now on I don't care for anything other than You. I don't care for my education, my work, or my future. I don't even care for my family or my own life. Lord Jesus, I care only for You." This is to be dead to everything in order to live to God.

As those who are dead to the law and alive to God, we have Christ living in us. In 2:20 Paul says, "I am crucified with Christ; and it is no longer I who live, but it is Christ who lives in me." This also is a basic aspect of the truth of the gospel. (*Life-study of Galatians,* pp. 75-76)

Further Reading: Life-study of Galatians, msg. 8

Enlightenment and inspiration: _____
_____
_____
_____

Morning Nourishment

Col. **Of which I became a minister according to the
1:25 stewardship of God, which was given to me for
you, to complete the word of God.**

Rom. **Paul, a slave of Christ Jesus, a called apostle, sepa-
1:1 rated unto the gospel of God.**

9 **For God is my witness, whom I serve in my spirit in
the gospel of His Son, how unceasingly I make
mention of you always in my prayers.**

12:5 **So we who are many are one Body in Christ, and
individually members one of another.**

Mark is the gospel of service. According to this Gospel, Christ
came as a slave to serve God by caring for God's people. Christ
came, not to be ministered unto, but to minister, to serve (10:45).
He came...as a slave to serve God by ministering to His redeemed people. Thus, Mark emphasizes service.

Paul's gospel includes all the aspects of the first four Gospels.
In his writings Paul speaks of the kingdom, life, forgiveness, and
service. However, in his Epistles he covers much more. In
Colossians 1:25 Paul says that he became a minister according
to the stewardship of God to complete the word of God. Hence,
Paul's gospel is the gospel of completion. Without Paul's gospel,
the revelation of the gospel in the New Testament would not be
complete. (*Life-study of Galatians*, p. 14)

Today's Reading

Many important aspects of the gospel are found only in the
writings of Paul. For example, in Colossians 1:27 Paul says that
Christ in us is the hope of glory. Such a word cannot be found in
the four Gospels, nor in the Epistles written by Peter or John.
Mark may be regarded as Peter's spiritual son (1 Pet. 5:13), and
he drew upon Peter as the source for much of the material in his
Gospel. However, Mark says nothing about the indwelling
Christ as our hope of glory. From Paul's gospel we learn that the
Spirit of Christ is a seal and a pledge (Eph. 1:13-14). Although
John speaks of the Spirit, he does not use the same terms Paul

does. In Galatians 1:15 and 16 Paul tells us that it pleased God to reveal His Son in him. Such a word is not to be found in Matthew, Mark, Luke, or John. Paul also speaks of Christ living in us (Gal. 2:20), of Christ being formed in us (4:19), and of Christ making His home in us (Eph. 3:17). Statements like these are not found in the four Gospels. Furthermore, in Ephesians 3:19 Paul speaks of being filled unto all the fullness of God. Matthew, Mark, Luke, and John have nothing to say about this.

In his Epistles Paul also tells us that we are members of the Body of Christ. He speaks of Christ as the Head and of the church as the Body. Such terms cannot be found in the writings of Peter or John. If we could tell Peter that the church is the Body of Christ, he might reply, "Where did you hear this? I was close to the Lord Jesus for three and a half years, but I never heard such a word. I heard about the cross and about feeding the Lord's lambs. In my first Epistle I even charged the elders to shepherd the flock of God. But I have never heard about the Body of Christ." We must admit that concerning the matter of the Head and the Body, Paul's vision was higher than Peter's. Although John tells us that Christ is the vine and that we are the branches, he does not say that Christ is the Head and that we are the Body. This is a further indication that without Paul's gospel the revelation in the New Testament would not be complete.

It is crucial for us to see that Paul's ministry was a completing ministry, a ministry of completing the divine revelation. Paul's gospel is the gospel of completion. Therefore, if we did not have Paul's writings, we would lack a vital part of God's revelation. Paul's Epistles not only complete the divine revelation; they form the very heart of God's revelation in the New Testament. Thus, Paul's gospel is not only the gospel of completion; it is also the center of the New Testament revelation. For this reason, Paul's gospel is the basic gospel. (*Life-study of Galatians,* pp. 14-16)

Further Reading: Life-study of Galatians, msg. 2, 34; *Crystallization-study of the Epistles to the Romans,* msg. 26

Enlightenment and inspiration: _____
_____
_____
_____

Morning Nourishment

Gal. To reveal His Son in me that I might announce Him
1:16 as the gospel among the Gentiles, immediately I
did not confer with flesh and blood.
3:26-27 For you are all sons of God through faith in Christ
Jesus. For as many of you as were baptized into
Christ have put on Christ.
4:19 My children, with whom I travail again in birth
until Christ is formed in you.

Paul was in travail that Christ might be formed in the Galatians [4:19]. Christ, a living person, is the focus of Paul's gospel. His
preaching is to bring forth Christ, the Son of the living God, in the
believers. This differs greatly from the teaching of the law in letters. Hence, the book of Galatians is emphatically Christ-centered.
Christ was crucified (3:1) to redeem us out of the curse of the law
(3:13) and rescue us out of the evil religious course of the world
(1:4); and He was resurrected from among the dead (1:1) that He
might live in us (2:20). We were baptized into Him, identified with
Him, and have put on Him, have clothed ourselves with Him (3:27).
Thus, we are in Him (3:28) and have become His (3:29; 5:24). On
the other hand, He has been revealed in us (1:16), He is now living
in us (2:20), and He will be formed in us (4:19). It is to Him the law
has conducted us (3:24), and in Him we are all sons of God (3:26). It
is in Him that we inherit God's promised blessing and enjoy the
all-inclusive Spirit (3:14). It is also in Him that we are all one (3:28).
We should not be deprived of all profit from Him and so be severed
from Him (5:4). We need Him to supply us with His grace in our spirit
(6:18) that we may live Him. (*Life-study of Galatians*, pp. 204-205)

Today's Reading

We in the Lord's recovery need to have a clear view of the gospel
according to Paul. The focal point of Paul's gospel is that the Son of
God, God's anointed One, has entered into our being to be our life
today and our glory in the future so that we may be the members of
His Body. This Body, the fullness of the One who fills all in all, is the
new man, the household of God, the household of faith, and the

true Israel of God. In Paul's gospel there are many mysterious matters that are not covered by Matthew, Mark, Luke, or John. In the four Gospels we are not told that Christ is the mystery of God (Col. 2:2) or that all the fullness of the Godhead dwells in Him bodily (Col. 2:9). In fact, the four Gospels do not even give us a clear word concerning justification by faith. It is in Romans and Galatians that justification by faith is covered in a clear way.

According to the revelation given to Paul, the gospel is…focused on the Triune God being our life in order to be one with us and to make us one with Him, that we may be the Body of Christ to express God in a corporate way. The focal point of the gospel is…God Himself in His Trinity becoming the processed all-inclusive Spirit to be life and everything to us for our enjoyment, so that He and we may be one to express Him for eternity. Such a profound thought cannot be found in the four Gospels.

Many Christians today are not clear about this matter either. They may be familiar with the councils, the creeds, and the teachings of the historic church, but they do not know Paul's revelation of the Triune God processed to become the all-inclusive Spirit.

Important aspects of Paul's gospel are found in Galatians. We have seen that in 1:15 and 16 Paul says that it pleased God to reveal His Son in him. What a wonderful word! However, millions of Christians have no realization that Christ is in them. In 2:20 Paul goes on to speak of Christ living in us, and in 4:19, of Christ being formed in us. In chapter six he covers fourteen important items: the human spirit (vv. 1, 18), the law of Christ (the law of life, v. 2), the Spirit (v. 8), eternal life (v. 8), the household (v. 10), the faith (v. 10), the cross of Christ (v. 14), the religious world, which has been crucified to Paul and to which Paul has been crucified (v. 14), the new creation (v. 15), peace (v. 16), mercy (v. 16), the Israel of God (v. 16), the brands of Jesus (v. 17), and the grace of Christ (v. 18). A number of these items can be found only in the writings of Paul, not in any of the four Gospels. (*Life-study of Galatians,* pp. 16-17)

Further Reading: Life-study of Galatians, msg. 2, 23

Enlightenment and inspiration: _____

_____

_____

_____

Hymns, #496

1　Christ is the one reality of all,
　Of Godhead and of man and all things else;
　No man without Him ever findeth God,
　Without Him man and everything is false.

2　All types and figures of the ancient time,
　All things we ever need, both great and small,
　Only are shadows of the Christ of God,
　Showing that He must be our all in all.

3　All things are vanity of vanities,
　Christ, the reality all things to fill;
　Though everything we may enjoy and own,
　If we're devoid of Christ we're empty still.

4　Christ is our real God, our real Lord,
　Christ is our real life, our real light;
　Christ is our real food, our real drink,
　Our real clothing, and our real might.

5　Christ also is the one reality
　Of all our doctrine and theology;
　And all our scriptural knowledge without Him
　Is just in letter and is vanity.

6　Christ, the reality of time and space,
　Christ, the reality of every stage;
　Christ is the one reality of all
　Thru all eternity from age to age.

Composition for prophecy with main point and sub-points: _____

_____
_____
_____
_____
_____
_____
_____
_____
_____
_____
_____
_____
_____
_____
_____
_____
_____
_____
_____
_____
_____
_____
_____
_____
_____
_____
_____
_____
_____
_____
_____
_____

A Revelation of God's Economy—
"I" Crucified in Christ's Death, and Christ
Living in Me in His Resurrection

Scripture Reading: Gal. 2:19-20; 1 Cor. 6:17; John 14:19; 15:4

Day 1   I. **Paul wrote the book of Galatians both according to truth and according to experience (2:5, 14; 4:16; 5:7; 1:15-16; 2:20; 4:19).**

II. **The Christian life is a life of organic oneness with Christ (John 15:4; Gal. 2:19-20):**

A. God desires that the divine life and the human life be joined to become one life; this oneness is a union in life (1 Cor. 6:17).

B. The Christian life is not an exchanged life—the exchange of a lower life for a higher one—but a grafted life—the grafting of the human life into the divine life and the mingling of the human life with the divine life (Rom. 11:24):

1. In grafting, two similar lives are joined and then grow together organically; in the process of spiritual grafting, two lives—the divine life and the human life—are grafted and become one (Gen. 1:26; 2:7).

2. In order for us to be grafted into Christ, He had to pass through the processes of incarnation, human living, crucifixion, and resurrection to become the life-giving Spirit (John 1:14; Matt. 1:1; 1 Cor. 15:45b).

3. When the preciousness of the Lord Jesus was infused into us and we began to appreciate Him, we were grafted into Him; we were joined to Christ in His resurrection and were organically united with Him (1 Cor. 6:17):

a. By believing into Christ and being baptized into Him, we have been grafted into

Him (John 3:15; Gal. 3:27).

b. We have been grafted into the One who is the seed to fulfill God's promise and also the life-giving Spirit as the blessing of the good land (vv. 16, 14).

Day 2
4. As regenerated ones, we should live a grafted life (John 15:4):

a. After we have been grafted into Christ, we should no longer live by ourselves; rather, we should allow the pneumatic Christ to live in us (Gal. 2:20).

b. We should no longer live by our flesh or by our natural being; instead, we should live by our regenerated spirit, a spirit grafted with Christ (1 Cor. 6:17).

5. In the grafted life, the divine life works to discharge the negative elements and to resurrect our God-created being (1 Thes. 5:23; Rom. 8:10, 6, 11).

6. Through this grafting, we are united, mingled, and incorporated with Christ to become in Him an enlarged, universal, divine and human incorporation—the Body of Christ, which consummates the New Jerusalem (1 Cor. 6:17; John 15:4; 14:20; Rev. 21:2).

Day 3
III. **In the organic union with Christ, we have the experience of being dead to the law and alive to God (Gal. 2:19):**

A. To be dead to the law means to be discharged from the law in which we were held; to live to God means to be obligated to God in the divine life (Rom. 7:6):

1. In Christ's death our obligation under the law has been terminated (v. 4a).

2. In Christ's resurrection we are responsible to God in the resurrection life (v. 4b).

B. If we are not actually organically united with Christ but are in ourselves, then we are neither dead to the law nor alive to God (1 Cor. 1:30; Gal. 2:16-17):

1. To be dead to the law and alive to God implies the death and resurrection of Christ (Rom. 6:3-5; Col. 2:12).
2. Only by being grafted into Christ to have an organic union with Him can we be one with Him in His death and resurrection.

C. In the organic union with Christ, His history becomes our history (Gal. 2:20):

1. One aspect of our history includes the crucifixion by which we have been cut off from everything other than God (6:14).
2. Another aspect of our history includes the resurrection in which we have been united with the Triune God (Rom. 6:5; Matt. 28:19).

D. When we are cut off from the law by means of the organic union with Christ, we spontaneously live to God (Gal. 2:19).

E. Because we and Christ are one, whatever belongs to Him is ours; through our organic union with Him, we share whatever He is and has (Eph. 3:8).

Day 4 **IV. In Galatians 2:20 we see the most basic truth of God's New Testament economy—no longer I but Christ living in me:**

A. According to God's economy, we should no longer live; rather, Christ should live in us:

1. God's economy is that "I" be crucified with Christ and that Christ live in me in His resurrection.
2. In His economy God's intention is for the processed Triune God to be wrought into our being to make us a new person, a new "I."

Day 5 & Day 6 B. As regenerated people we have both an old "I" and a new "I"; the old "I" has been terminated, but the new "I" lives:

1. The "I" who has been terminated is the "I" who was without divinity.

2. The "I" who still lives is the "I" into which God has been added.

3. The old "I" had nothing of God in it, whereas the new "I" has received the divine life.

4. The old "I" has become the new "I" because God as life has been added to it.

5. The new "I" is the "I" who came into being when the old "I" was resurrected and had God added to it.

C. We and Christ do not have two lives; rather, we have one life and one living:

1. We live by Him, and He lives in us (John 6:57).

2. If we do not live, He does not live, and if He does not live, we cannot live.

3. Christ lives in us by causing and enabling us to live with Him (14:19).

D. "I," the natural person, is inclined to keep the law that I might be perfect (Phil. 3:6), but God wants me to live Christ that God may be expressed in me through Him; hence, God's economy is that "I" be crucified in Christ's death and that Christ live in me in His resurrection.

Morning Nourishment

Gal. For I through law have died to law that I might live
2:19 to God.
Rom. For if we have grown together with *Him* in the like-
6:5 ness of His death, indeed we will also be *in the likeness*
of His resurrection.
7:4 So then, my brothers, you also have been made dead
to the law through the body of Christ so that you
might be joined to another, to Him who has been
raised from the dead, that we might bear fruit to God.
11:16-17 ...And if the root is holy, the branches are also. But...
you, being a wild olive tree, were grafted in among
them and became a fellow partaker of the root of fatness of the olive tree.

Galatians 2:19 indicates that we have already died to law. According to your experience, have you actually died to law, or is this
simply a matter of doctrine to you? Furthermore, how can we live
to God? If we would answer these questions, we must know the
truth, the reality, of the gospel. If we are not actually organically
united with Christ but are in ourselves, then we are neither dead
to law nor are we living to God. Apart from the organic union with
Christ, we cannot live to God. On the contrary, we shall be alive to
many things other than God.

The concept of organic union is implied in Romans 7 [where]...
Paul uses the illustration of married life. Marriage is a union of life.
In this union the wife is one with the husband, and the husband is
one with the wife. In Romans 7:4,...we have been married to the
resurrected Christ. Between Him as the Bridegroom and us as the
bride, there is a wonderful union. We are one with Him in person,
name, life, and existence. This shows that our Christian life is a life
of organic oneness with Christ. (*Life-study of Galatians,* pp. 77-78)

Today's Reading

In Romans 11 Paul goes on to use another illustration—the
grafting of a branch from one tree into another tree....As a result of
grafting, the branches from the wild olive tree and the cultivated

olive tree grow together organically. We, branches of the wild olive tree, have been grafted into Christ, the cultivated olive tree.

Once we were wild olive branches, but now we have been grafted into Christ. This illustration indicates that the Christian life is not an exchanged life, the exchange of a lower life for a higher one, but a grafted life, the grafting of the human life into the life of Christ. After a branch has been grafted into another tree, it no longer lives by itself. On the contrary, it lives by the tree into which it has been grafted.

In the matter of grafting, there are two main aspects: cutting and joining or uniting. Without the cutting, there cannot be any grafting. If the branch from one tree is to be grafted into another tree, the branch must firstly be cut. After the cutting occurs, the joining or union takes place. This union is organic. Therefore, in grafting we have the cutting, the joining, and the organic union. The cutting corresponds to the death of Christ, and the uniting, to the resurrection of Christ. In the death of Christ our old life was cut off, and in Christ's resurrection we were united to Him for further growth. The experience of the death of Christ causes us to die to the law, whereas resurrection enables us to live to God. Hence, to be dead to the law and alive to God implies the death and resurrection of Christ. Only by being grafted into Christ can we be one with Him in His death and resurrection.

In ourselves it is not possible for us to die to law or live to God. However, when the preciousness of the Lord Jesus was infused into us and we began to appreciate Him, we were grafted into Him. On the one hand, we were cut; on the other hand, we were joined to Christ in His resurrection life. After this union took place, we were organically united with Christ. Now we should simply live in this organic union. On the negative side, we have been cut in Christ's death; on the positive side, we have been united to Christ in His resurrection. (*Life-study of Galatians,* pp. 78-79)

Further Reading: Life-study of Galatians, msgs. 8-9, 16, 20, 22, 25; *Life Messages,* chs. 58-59; *Life-study of Romans,* msgs. 63-65

Enlightenment and inspiration: _____

_____

_____

_____

Morning Nourishment

John   Abide in Me and I in you. As the branch cannot bear
15:4   fruit of itself unless it abides in the vine, so neither
       can you unless you abide in Me.
14:20 In that day you will know that I am in My Father,
       and you in Me, and I in you.
1 Cor. But he who is joined to the Lord is one spirit.
6:17

Within you, you probably prefer to have [the Lord] with you, as He was with the early disciples. If the Lord Jesus would suddenly appear in a physical way, we would be amazed. This proves that we prefer a Christ among us to a Christ in us. However, if Christ were still just among us, His life could not be grafted together with ours, because He would not be in us. He could perform miracles among us, but we would remain the same, without change or transformation. We could embrace Him, but we could not be grafted into Him. Therefore, in order that we may be mingled with Him, Christ prefers to be in us. He wants us to abide in Him so that He may abide in us (John 15:4). This is the mingling that produces the grafted life. It is this life that transforms us and conforms us to the image of Christ.

In order to be qualified to enter into us, Christ had to pass through incarnation, human living, crucifixion, resurrection, and ascension. Furthermore, as the Spirit, He had to descend upon us. Then the only thing remaining is for us to call upon Him in faith. When we say, "O Lord Jesus, I believe in You," His qualified life enters into our prepared life, and the two lives are joined. In this way our life is grafted into His. (*Life-study of Romans*, pp. 670-671)

Today's Reading

This word concerning our being grafted with Christ may be simple, yet what is involved includes the heaven, the earth, and many other things. Here it says that we have been grafted into Christ, yet this Christ is the God who dwells in unapproachable light (1 Tim. 6:16). Since we cannot touch Him, how can we be grafted into Him? This is why Christ needed to pass through various processes. The first process that He went through was His becoming flesh (John 1:14) to be the seed of David (Matt. 1:1), the branch of David (Zech. 3:8; Jer. 23:5; 33:15), that we might be grafted together with Him. As human beings we are branches, pieces of wood; in like manner, Christ came as the branch of David, as a piece of wood. He is exactly the same as we are; hence, He and we can be grafted together.

A grafter knows that in order to have a successful grafting, both of the grafting parts need to be cut and die....On Christ's side, one day, as the branch of David, He died on the cross; however, although He died in the flesh, He was resurrected in the Spirit (1 Pet. 3:18b). Through death and resurrection He became the life-giving Spirit (1 Cor. 15:45b). By becoming such a Spirit, Christ was ready for the grafting. On our side, as sinners, we need to repent and receive the Lord. Once we repent and receive Him, He as the life-giving Spirit enters into our spirit and puts the divine life in us. This life is a life of death and resurrection. Hence, He brings the key to death and resurrection into us who have believed in Him and have died and resurrected with Him. Thus, in this death and resurrection we are grafted together with Christ.

After we have been grafted together with Christ, we should no longer live by ourselves; rather, we should allow the pneumatic Christ to live in us. Furthermore, we should no longer live by our flesh or our natural being; rather, we should live by our mingled spirit, a spirit grafted with Christ. Thus, first, we are united with Him; this is a union. Then we are mingled with Him; this is a mingling. Eventually, we are incorporated with Him into an incorporation. This incorporation is the New Jerusalem, the great universal incorporation of the mingling of God and man for us to reign in eternity. (*The Experience of God's Organic Salvation Equaling Reigning in Christ's Life,* pp. 51-52)

Further Reading: Life-study of Romans, msgs. 63-65; *The Experience of God's Organic Salvation Equaling Reigning in Christ's Life,* msg. 4

Enlightenment and inspiration: _____

_____

_____

_____

Morning Nourishment

Gal. 2:19 For I through law have died to law that I might live to God.

6:14 But far be it from me to boast except in the cross of our Lord Jesus Christ, through whom the world has been crucified to me and I to the world.

Rom. 6:4 We have been buried therefore with Him through baptism into His death, in order that just as Christ was raised from the dead through the glory of the Father, so also we might walk in newness of life.

According to Galatians 6, we are dead to the world, particularly to the religious world, through the crucifixion of Christ (vv. 13-14). By the all-inclusive cutting of Christ's all-inclusive death on the cross, we are dead to everything other than God. Because we have been grafted into Christ, His experience has become our history. When He died on the cross, we died in Him. When He was crucified, we were cut off from the wild olive tree. This means that we were cut off from the self, the flesh, the world, religion, and the law with its ordinances. Furthermore, because we have been grafted into Christ, His resurrection has also become our history. Therefore, we can strongly declare that with Christ we have been crucified, buried, and resurrected. What a wonderful history we have! (*Life-study of Galatians,* p. 79)

Today's Reading

Whenever we say from the depths of our heart, "Lord Jesus, I love You," our faith is strengthened. Our organic union with Christ is strengthened also. Furthermore, we sense that we have been cut away from sin, the world, the flesh, and religion. Some who have seen the light concerning the church have not been willing to give up the denominations. But one day they told the Lord how much they loved Him. Spontaneously they had the sense within that they should give up their association with the denominations. Because their organic union with Christ was strengthened, they experienced more cutting. The more we say, "Lord

Jesus, I love You," the more we sense that we have been cut off from everything other than Christ.

In 2:19 Paul says, "For I through law have died to law that I might live to God." The law requires me, a sinner, to die, and according to that requirement Christ died for me and with me. Hence, I have died in Christ and with Christ through the law. Therefore, the obligation under the law, the relationship to the law, has been terminated. To live to God means to be obligated to God in the divine life. In Christ's death we are through with the law, and in His resurrection we are responsible to God in the resurrection life.

To be dead to law means that we have been discharged from the law in which we were held [Rom. 7:6]....Having been liberated from obligation to the law, we may now walk in newness of life (Rom. 6:4). However, walking in newness of life depends upon the cutting we experience in the organic union with Christ. The more we experience the cutting, the more we live to God and walk in newness of life. Because we have died to law, we are no longer obligated to keep the law by the striving of the flesh (Gal. 3:3). Whenever we have a certain self-made law, we always strive to keep it by the strength of the flesh, not by the Spirit.

To be living unto God is to be obligated to God in the divine life, to be responsible to God in the resurrection life. In the organic union with Christ, we experience resurrection life. In this resurrection life we are held to God spontaneously and are obligated to Him. This also depends on the organic union.

Because we have been crucified with Christ, it is no longer we who live, but Christ lives in us. We no longer live in the old man, the natural man. Rather, Christ lives in us. Then in resurrection we live in the faith of the Son of God. To live in the faith of the Son of God means to live in the organic union with the Son of God which comes through our believing in Him. (*Life-study of Galatians,* pp. 80-81, 83-84)

Further Reading: Life-study of Galatians, msgs. 8-9; *Elders' Training, Book 6: The Crucial Points of the Truth in Paul's Epistles,* ch. 5

Enlightenment and inspiration: _____

_____

_____

_____

Morning Nourishment

Gal. I am crucified with Christ; and *it is* no longer I *who*
2:20 live, but *it is* Christ *who* lives in me; and the *life* which
I now live in the flesh I live in faith, the *faith* of the
Son of God, who loved me and gave Himself up for me.
4:19 My children, with whom I travail again in birth until
Christ is formed in you.

Galatians 2:20 is a familiar verse. In this verse is one of the
basic items of God's New Testament economy: no longer I, but
Christ living in me. According to God's economy, we should no longer live; rather, Christ should live in us. This is a basic aspect of
the truth of the gospel. However, most Christians do not have the
proper and adequate understanding of what it means to say no
longer I, but Christ living in me.

The Galatians had turned from God's economy and had gone
back to the law, which they were trying to keep by the efforts of the
flesh. But when we endeavor to keep the law in this way, we are far
off from God. God's economy is not that we try to keep the law in
the strength of our flesh. His economy is to work Himself into us.
The Triune God has become the processed God. Through incarnation, Christ came in the flesh to fulfill the law and then to set it
aside. Through His resurrection, Christ has become the life-giving
Spirit, ready to enter into us. God's New Testament economy is for
the processed Triune God to be wrought into us to become our life
and our very being. If we see this, we shall be able to proclaim that
we have been crucified with Christ and that we live no longer. Nevertheless Christ lives in us, and we live by the faith that is in Him
and of Him. Our old person has been crucified, but the new person,
the new "I," still lives. Now we live by faith in the Son of God and of
the Son of God, a faith that produces an organic union in which we
and Christ are one. There is no comparison between keeping the
law and such an organic union. (*Life-study of Galatians,* pp. 85, 93)

Today's Reading

Galatians 2:20 is a revelation of God's economy. In His economy
God's intention is for the processed Triune God to be wrought into

our being to make us a new person, a new "I." The old person, the old "I," the "I" without God, is over; but the new person, the new "I," the "I" with the Triune God in it, still lives. We live with Christ and by Christ. Furthermore, we live by faith, which is the means to bring us into oneness with Him. In this organic union we are one with the Lord, for we have one life and one living with Him. When we live, He lives. He lives in us, and we live with Him.

I believe that now we can understand what it means to say that Christ lives in us and that the life which we now live, we live by the faith of the Son of God who loved us and gave Himself for us. The experience portrayed in this verse implies that God in His Trinity has been processed. After Christ was incarnated, He lived on earth and then was crucified, buried, and resurrected. In resurrection He became the life-giving Spirit. After His ascension, Christ was crowned, enthroned, and made the Lord of all. On the day of Pentecost, He descended as the Spirit upon His Body. From that time until now, He has been working and moving on earth, seeking those who will appreciate Him and call on His name. Whenever we call on the Lord Jesus out of our appreciation of Him, He comes into us and becomes the living faith which operates in us and brings us into an organic union with Him. In this union we can truly say, "I am crucified with Christ; and it is no longer I who live, but it is Christ who lives in me; and the life which I now live in the flesh I live in faith, the faith of the Son of God, who loved me and gave Himself up for me." This is God's New Testament economy.

I can testify that because I have seen this heavenly vision, nothing can move me. I am willing to give my whole life for such a vision of God's economy. The old person has been crucified with Christ, and Christ now lives in me, the new person. The life I now live, I live by faith, the faith of the Son of God and in the Son of God, who loved me and gave Himself for me. Here we have the mingling of the Triune God with the tripartite man. How wonderful! (*Life-study of Galatians*, pp. 93-94)

Further Reading: Life-study of Galatians, msg. 10

Enlightenment and inspiration: _____

_____

_____

_____

Morning Nourishment

Gal.
2:19-20

For I through law have died to law that I might live to God. I am crucified with Christ; and *it is* no longer I *who* live, but *it is* Christ *who* lives in me; and the *life* which I now live in the flesh I live in faith, the *faith* of the Son of God, who loved me and gave Himself up for me.

We have pointed out that the book of Galatians reveals the basic truths of God's New Testament economy. Among these basic truths, the most basic one is found in 2:20. Because the truth of no longer I, but Christ living in me is so basic, it is also mysterious; and because it is mysterious, it has not been properly understood by Christians throughout the centuries. Therefore, we look to the Lord that He would make this basic truth clear to us. (*Life-study of Galatians*, p. 86)

Today's Reading

We have pointed out that in this verse Paul says, on the one hand, "no longer I" and, on the other hand, "I now live." How can we reconcile this? Once again I wish to point out that this is not an exchange of life. The way to interpret the Bible properly is by the Bible itself. This means that other verses are needed if we are to understand this verse. Romans 6:6 tells us that our old man has been crucified with Christ. This verse helps us to see that the very I who has been crucified with Christ is the old "I," the old man. As regenerated people, we have both an old "I" and a new "I." The old "I" has been terminated, but the new "I" lives. In Galatians 2:20 we have both the old "I" and the new "I." The old "I" has been crucified with Christ, terminated. Therefore, Paul can say, "no longer I." However, the new "I" still lives. For this reason, Paul can say, "I live."

Now we must go on to see the difference between the old "I" and the new "I." Because we are so familiar with 2:20, we may take this verse for granted and assume that we understand it.

[handwritten at top: the processed Triune God is bringing Himself fully into us that He may be our realm like the good land which was to Israel]

But what is the difference between the old "I" and the new "I"? According to the natural understanding, some would say that the old "I" is evil, whereas the new "I" is good. This concept of the difference between the old "I" and the new "I" must be rejected. The old "I" had nothing of God in it, whereas the new "I" has received the divine life. The old "I" has become a new "I" because God as life has been added to it. The "I" that has been terminated is the "I" that was without divinity. The "I" who still lives is the "I" into which God has been added. There is a great difference here. The old "I," the "I" without God, has been terminated. But the new "I" still lives, the "I" that came into being when the old "I" was resurrected and had God added to it. On the one hand, Paul has been terminated. But, on the other hand, a resurrected Paul, one with God as his life, still lives.

[handwritten right margin: no longer an old I, old man only a new I, a new man with God as life in it.]

Because of their rejection of God's light many Christians are blind to this understanding of 2:20. If they heard such a word about the old "I" and the new "I," they would reject it. Their rejection, however, would be completely without ground. As genuine Christians, they have been regenerated. When a person is regenerated, he is not annihilated or destroyed. To be regenerated means to have God added into us. In regeneration, we who once did not have God in us now have Him added to us. The very "I" who did not have God in it is over. This is the old "I," the old man, who has been crucified with Christ. But from the time that we began to appreciate the Lord Jesus and the operating faith began to work in us, this faith brought the processed Triune God into us and added Him to our being. From that time onward, we have had a new "I," an "I" with God in it. Hence, the new "I" is the old "I" which has become an "I" resurrected with God added to it. Praise the Lord that the old "I" has been terminated and the new "I" now lives! (*Life-study of Galatians,* pp. 86-87)

Further Reading: Life-study of Galatians, msgs. 10, 41

Enlightenment and inspiration: *[handwritten: faith and love are two tender things that keep us in union with the resurrected Christ who is life to us. This is a heart matter. How we need to care for, guard, our heart]*

Morning Nourishment

John As the living Father has sent Me and I live because of
6:57   the Father, so he who eats Me, he also shall live be-
       cause of Me.
14:19 Yet a little while and the world beholds Me no longer,
       but you behold Me; because I live, you also shall live.
Phil. As to zeal, persecuting the church; as to the right-
3:6   eousness which is in the law, become blameless.

In Galatians 2:20 Paul says, "Christ...lives in me." According to
the concept of an exchanged life, our life is terminated and Christ lives.
But we need a more thorough understanding of what it means to say
that Christ lives *in us.* It is rather easy to understand that Christ lives.
But it is difficult to understand how Christ lives in us. This does not
mean that I have been crucified and live no longer, and that Christ
lives instead of me. On the one hand, Paul said, "No longer I"; on the
other hand, he said, "Christ...lives in me." The phrase *in me* is of great
importance. Yes, it is Christ who lives, but it is in us that He lives.

In order to understand how Christ can live in us, we need to
turn to John 14. Before His death and resurrection, the Lord Jesus
said to the disciples, "Because I live, you also shall live" (v. 19).
Christ lives in us by causing us to live with Him. Christ does not
live alone. He lives in us and with us. He lives by enabling us to live
with Him. In a very real sense, if we do not live with Him, He cannot live in us. We have not been altogether ruled out, and our life
has not been exchanged for the divine life. We continue to exist, but
we exist with the Triune God. The Triune God who now dwells
within us causes us to live with Christ. Hence, Christ lives in us
through our living with Him. (*Life-study of Galatians,* pp. 87-88)

Today's Reading

Once again the illustration of grafting helps our understanding.
After a branch has been grafted into a productive tree, the branch
continues to live. However, it lives not by itself, but by the tree into
which it has been grafted. Furthermore, the tree lives in the branch
which has been grafted into it. The branch now lives a grafted life.
This means that it lives, not by itself, but by the life of the tree into

which it has been grafted. Furthermore, this other life, the life of the productive tree, does not live by itself, but through the branch grafted into it. The life of the tree lives in the branch. Eventually, the branch and the tree have one life with one living. In the same principle, we and Christ also have one life and one living.

In John 6:57 the Lord Jesus said, "As the living Father has sent Me, and I live because of the Father, so he who eats Me, he also shall live because of Me." The Son did not live by Himself. However, this does not mean that the Son was set aside and ceased to exist. The Son, of course, continued to exist, but He did not live His own life. Instead, He lived the life of the Father. In this way the Son and the Father had one life and one living. They shared the same life and had the same living.

It is the same in our relationship with Christ today. We and Christ do not have two lives. Rather, we have one life and one living. We live by Him, and He lives in us. If we do not live, He does not live; and if He does not live, we cannot live. On the one hand, we are terminated; on the other hand, we continue to exist, but we do not live without Him. Christ lives within us, and we live with Him. Therefore, we and He have one life and one living.

Galatians 2:20 explains how through law we have died to law. When Christ was crucified, we were included in Him according to God's economy. This is an accomplished fact. We have died in Christ through His death, but now He lives in us through His resurrection. His living in us is entirely by His being the life-giving Spirit (1 Cor. 15:45b). This point is fully developed in the following chapters of Galatians, where the Spirit is presented and emphasized as the very One whom we have received as life and in whom we should live.

"I," the natural person, is inclined to keep the law that I might be perfect (Phil. 3:6), but God wants me to live Christ that God may be expressed in me through Him (Phil. 1:20-21). Hence, God's economy is that "I" be crucified in Christ's death and Christ live in me in His resurrection. (*Life-study of Galatians*, pp. 88-89)

Further Reading: Life-study of Galatians, msg. 10

Enlightenment and inspiration: _____

_____

_____

_____

Hymns, #482

1   I am crucified with Christ,
    And the cross hath set me free;
    I have ris'n again with Christ,
    And He lives and reigns in me.

      Oh! it is so sweet to die with Christ,
      To the world, and self, and sin;
      Oh! it is so sweet to live with Christ,
      As He lives and reigns within.

2   Mystery hid from ancient ages!
    But at length to faith made plain:
    Christ in me the Hope of Glory,
    Tell it o'er and o'er again.

3   This the secret nature hideth,
    Harvest grows from buried grain;
    A poor tree with better grafted,
    Richer, sweeter life doth gain.

4   This the secret of the holy,
    Not our holiness, but Him;
    O Lord! empty us and fill us,
    With Thy fulness to the brim.

5   This the balm for pain and sickness,
    Just to all our strength to die,
    And to find His life and fulness,
    All our being's need supply.

6   This the story of the Master,
    Thru the Cross, He reached the Throne,
    And like Him our path to glory,
    Ever leads through death alone.

Composition for prophecy with main point and sub-points: _____

_____

_____

_____

_____

_____

_____

_____

_____

_____

_____

_____

_____

_____

_____

_____

_____

_____

_____

_____

_____

_____

_____

_____

_____

_____

_____

_____

_____

_____

_____

_____

_____

Not Nullifying the Grace of God
but Receiving and Enjoying
the Grace of God in Our Spirit

Scripture Reading: Gal. 2:20-21; 5:4; 3:2, 5; 6:17-18

Day 1 I. **God's eternal economy is for His people to enjoy Him as the Triune God who has been processed to become the life-giving Spirit through incarnation, human living, crucifixion, resurrection, and ascension so that they might be constituted with Him for His corporate expression today in the church life and in the next age and for eternity in the New Jerusalem (Eph. 3:8-11; cf. Rev. 1:11-12; 21:2).**

II. **Grace is Christ Himself, the embodiment of the Triune God, as the life-giving Spirit for our enjoyment; to nullify the grace of God means that in our experience we deny Christ the opportunity to live in us and do not live by the Spirit (John 1:1, 14, 16-17; Gal. 2:20; 1 Cor. 15:10, 45b; Gal. 2:21; 4:19; 5:25; cf. Col. 2:19):**

Day 2 A. To go back to the law is to reject this grace, to nullify this grace, to fall from grace (Gal. 2:21; 5:4):

1. To fall from grace is to be brought to nought, reduced to nothing, separated from Christ, deprived of all profit from Christ (cf. John 15:4-5).

2. The present evil, religious age keeps people away from the real enjoyment of Christ; the Lord's recovery is to recover Christ as everything to us for our enjoyment (Gal. 1:4; 2 Cor. 11:2-3; 1 Cor. 1:9).

3. If we go to anything other than Christ, such as the law or character improvement, and do not cleave to Christ that we may enjoy Him all the time, our enjoyment of Christ will be confiscated (cf. Col. 2:18).

B. We need to stand fast in the grace into which we have entered (Rom. 5:1-2):
1. If we would be those who do not nullify the grace of God, we need to abide in Christ, which is to remain in the processed Triune God (John 15:4-5).
2. Furthermore, we need to enjoy Christ, especially by eating Him (6:57b).
3. Then we should go on to be one spirit with Christ (1 Cor. 6:17), to walk by the Spirit (Gal. 5:16, 25), to deny the natural "I" (2:20), and to abandon the flesh (5:24).

Day 3   C. Galatians begins with our being rescued from the present evil age, and it ends with the grace of the Lord with our spirit; we need to be rescued out of the present evil age of religion, which is mostly in our mind, to the wonderful enjoyment of Christ in our spirit (1:4; 6:18; John 4:24).

Day 4   III. **We need to be those who are receiving and enjoying the grace of the Lord in our spirit; the receiving of Christ as the Spirit of grace is a lifelong, continuous matter (John 1:16; Heb. 10:29b):**
A. Day by day a marvelous divine transmission should be taking place: God is supplying the Spirit of grace bountifully, and we should be receiving the Spirit of grace continually (Gal. 3:2-5; John 3:34):
1. The way to open ourselves to the heavenly transmission to receive the supply of the all-inclusive life-giving Spirit of grace is to exercise our spirit to pray and call on the Lord (1 Thes. 5:16-18; Rom. 10:12-13).
2. As we receive the Triune God as our grace and enjoy Him as grace, we shall gradually become one with Him organically; He will become our constituent, and we shall become His expression (2 Cor. 1:12; 12:9).

Day 5

B. The grace of the Lord Jesus Christ, the grace of
God, is the bountiful supply of the Triune God
(who is embodied in the Son and realized as the
life-giving Spirit) enjoyed by us through the exercise of our human spirit; grace is in our spirit
for our remaining in God's eternal economy
(Gal. 6:18):

1. Grace is the moving, acting, and anointing
   of the Spirit within us, and our spirit is the
   only place where we can experience grace
   (v. 18; Heb. 10:29b).

2. The way to receive and enjoy grace is to
   turn to the spirit, exercise the spirit, and
   enthrone the Lord:

   a. The throne of grace is in our spirit, and
      we need to receive the abundance of
      grace into our inward parts so that grace
      may reign within us for us to reign in life
      over Satan, sin, and death (Heb. 4:16;
      Rom. 5:17, 21; cf. Rev. 4:2).

   b. Whenever we come to the throne of grace
      by turning to our spirit and calling on the
      name of the Lord, we should enthrone
      the Lord, giving Him the headship, the
      kingship, and the lordship within us (Col
      1:18b; Rev. 2:4).

   c. God's throne is the source of the flowing
      grace; whenever we fail to enthrone the
      Lord, dethroning Him, the flow of grace
      stops (22:1).

   d. If we enthrone the Lord Jesus within us,
      the Spirit as the river of water of life will
      flow out from the throne of grace to sup-
      ply us; in this way we shall receive grace
      and enjoy grace (v. 1; *Hymns,* #770).

Day 6

IV. **As we bear the brands of Jesus, we enjoy the
grace of Christ (Gal. 6:17-18):**

A. The word *brands* in verse 17 refers to the marks
branded on slaves to indicate their owners; with

Paul, a slave of Christ (Rom. 1:1), the brands were physically the scars of his wounds received in his faithful service to his Master (2 Cor. 11:23-27).

B. Spiritually, the brands of Jesus signify the characteristics of the life that he lived, a life like the one the Lord Jesus lived on this earth; such a life is continually crucified (John 12:24), does the will of God (6:38), does not seek its own glory but the glory of God (7:18), and is submissive and obedient to God, even unto the death of the cross (Phil. 2:8).

C. If we bear the brands of Jesus and live a crucified life, we shall enjoy the grace of Christ as the supply of the life-giving Spirit in our spirit for us to minister Christ as God's grace to God's household (3:10; 2 Cor. 4:10-11; Eph. 3:2).

V. **The grace of the Lord Jesus dispensed to His believers throughout the New Testament age consummates in the New Jerusalem as the consummation of God's good pleasure in uniting, mingling, and incorporating Himself with man for His glorious enlargement and expression (Rev. 22:21; Eph. 2:10).**

Morning Nourishment

Gal. I am crucified with Christ; and *it is* no longer I *who*
2:20-21 live, but *it is* Christ *who* lives in me; and the *life* which
I now live in the flesh I live in faith, the *faith* of the
Son of God, who loved me and gave Himself up for
me. I do not nullify the grace of God; for if righteousness is through law, then Christ has died for nothing.

5:25 If we live by the Spirit, let us also walk by the Spirit.

In 2:21 Paul says, "I do not nullify the grace of God." If we consider this verse in context, we see that to nullify the grace of God
means that in our experience we do not have Christ living in us.
In verse 20 Paul says, "It is no longer I who live, but Christ lives in
me." Then he goes on to say that he does not nullify the grace of
God. This is a strong indication that for us as believers to nullify
the grace of God is for us to deny Christ the opportunity to live in
us. The grace of God is simply the living Christ Himself. To allow
Christ to live in us is to enjoy the grace of God. But not to allow
Him to live in us is to nullify God's grace. (*Life-study of Galatians,*
p. 95)

Today's Reading

Now we must give a definition of grace. Grace is God in His
Trinity processed through incarnation, human living, crucifixion,
resurrection, and ascension to be everything to us. After passing
through such a long process, the Triune God has become everything to us. He is our redemption, salvation, life, and sanctification. Having been processed to become the all-inclusive life-giving
Spirit, the Triune God Himself is our grace.

This description of what the grace of God is to us covers the entire New Testament from the opening of Matthew to the end of
Revelation. The Triune God—the Father, the Son, and the Spirit—
has been processed through incarnation, human living, crucifixion, resurrection, and ascension in order to come into us, to be one
with us, and to be everything to us. Now He is our redemption,
salvation, life, living, sanctification, and transformation, and He

will become our conformation, our glorification, and our eternity. This is the portion of the saints in light (Col. 1:12).

We cannot enjoy God's grace in full in one day or even in a lifetime. It will take eternity for us to have the full enjoyment of this grace. This is the very grace which came when the Lord Jesus came, and this is the grace we need day by day. Praise the Lord that this is the grace we find by approaching the throne of grace daily to meet our timely need. Every morning we should look to the Lord and pray, "Lord, grant me Your grace today. I need today's portion of Your grace. May grace be with me and with all my brothers and sisters." Oh, we all need to pray like this! Then we shall experience grace, the grace who is the very Triune God processed to become the all-inclusive life-giving Spirit for our enjoyment.

In Galatians 2:21 Paul says, "For if righteousness is through the law, then Christ has died for nothing." Christ died for us that we may have righteousness in Him, through which we may receive the divine life (Rom. 5:18, 21). This righteousness is not through the law, but through the death of Christ. If righteousness is through the law, Christ has died without cause, for nothing. But righteousness is through Christ's death, which has separated us from law. Now, according to Romans 5:17, we who "receive the abundance of grace and of the gift of righteousness will reign in life through the One, Jesus Christ." Grace enables us to reign in life.

It is the grace of God that Christ has imparted the divine life into us through the life-giving Spirit. Not to live by this Spirit is to nullify the grace of God. To nullify God's grace is to reject the processed Triune God who has become the all-inclusive life-giving Spirit. The Judaizers wanted the Galatian believers to go back to the law. To return to the law is to nullify the grace of God. It is to deny and reject the processed Triune God. Furthermore, it is also to fail to experience and enjoy such a processed God. By this we can see that to nullify the grace of God by returning to the law is extremely serious. (*Life-study of Galatians,* pp. 96, 99-100)

Further Reading: Life-study of Galatians, msg. 11

Enlightenment and inspiration: _____

_____

_____

_____

Morning Nourishment

Gal. You have been brought to nought, *separated* from
5:4 Christ, you who are being justified by law; you
have fallen from grace.
John Abide in Me and I in you. As the branch cannot
15:4-5 bear fruit of itself unless it abides in the vine, so
neither *can* you unless you abide in Me. I am the
vine; you are the branches. He who abides in Me
and I in him, he bears much fruit; for apart from
Me you can do nothing.

If we would be those who do not nullify the grace of God [Gal.
2:21], we need to abide in Christ (John 15:4-5). To abide in Christ
is to remain in the processed Triune God. Furthermore, we need
to enjoy Christ, especially by eating Him (John 6:57b). Then we
should go on to be one spirit with Christ (1 Cor. 6:17), to walk in
the Spirit (Gal. 5:16, 25), to deny the natural "I" (2:20), and to
abandon the flesh (5:24). We should not be distracted by things
such as the law, circumcision, the Sabbath, and dietary regulations. Rather, we should enjoy Christ and live with Him in one
spirit. If we walk in spirit, deny the natural "I," and abandon the
flesh, we shall be those who do not nullify the grace of God.
(*Life-study of Galatians*, p. 101)

Today's Reading

Different translations render the first part of Galatians 5:4 in
different ways: "Christ is become of no effect unto you" (KJV); "Ye
are severed from Christ" (ASV); "Ye are deprived of all profit from
the Christ" (Darby's New Translation). To be brought to nought
from Christ is to be reduced to nothing from Christ, deprived of all
profit from Christ and so separated from Him (Darby), so that He
is made void of effect. To go back to law is to become severed from
Christ, to be brought to nought from Christ.

In this verse Paul is talking about being brought to nothing, to
nought, from Christ. He was telling the Galatians, "Dear saints,
you who seek to be justified by law have been brought to nothing
from Christ. You were grafted into Christ, and you were enjoying

the riches of Christ. But by going back to the law and to circumcision, you are brought to nought, you are annihilated, from
Christ."

If a branch from an inferior tree is grafted into a superior tree,
it will enjoy all the benefits of being part of that superior tree. But
suppose the grafted branch is later detached from the superior
tree. In such a case we may say that it is brought to nothing from
the superior tree, for by being separated from that tree, it relin-
quishes all the benefits of being joined to it. Thus, it reduces itself
to nothing from the superior tree, in particular from the enjoyment of the riches of that tree. This illustrates Paul's meaning in
5:4. By believing into Christ and being baptized into Him, we
have been grafted into Him as the rich tree. As branches grafted
into Him, we may enjoy His unsearchable riches. As long as we
remain grafted into Him, we may enjoy all His riches. But if we
relinquish Christ, let Him go in a practical way in our experience,
we shall be brought to nothing from the unsearchably rich Christ.

The experience Paul presents in chapters three and four is actually related to our being grafted into Christ. We have been
grafted into the One who, on the one hand, is the seed to fulfill the
promise and, on the other hand, is the life-giving Spirit as the
blessing of the good land. Since our position is that of branches
grafted into Christ, we may enjoy all His riches. But if we go back
to the law, we shall detach ourselves from Christ as the superior
tree and be brought to nothing from Him. We shall be reduced to
nothing from the enjoyment of Christ. Then Christ will not profit
us anything, for we shall have fallen from grace....Have you been
detached from Christ? Have you been brought to nought from
Him, deprived of all the profit there is for you in Christ? I hope
that all of us in the Lord's recovery can strongly declare, "No, we
have not been brought to nothing from Christ! We abide in Him to
enjoy all He is to us." (*Life-study of Galatians*, pp. 221-224)

Further Reading: Life-study of Galatians, msgs. 11, 25; *Elders' Train-*
ing, Book 6: The Crucial Points of the Truth in Paul's Epistles, ch. 5

Enlightenment and inspiration: _____

_____

_____

_____

Morning Nourishment

Gal. Who gave Himself for our sins that He might rescue
1:4 us out of the present evil age according to the will of
our God and Father.
6:18 The grace of our Lord Jesus Christ be with your
spirit, brothers. Amen.
John God is Spirit, and those who worship Him must
4:24 worship in spirit and truthfulness.

The proper Christian life is nothing but a daily walk in Christ.
And today this Christ is the very Spirit within us for our experience. So this book begins with deliverance from this present evil
age, and it ends with this: "The grace of our Lord Jesus Christ be
with your spirit, brothers. Amen" (Gal 6:18).

Are we living in this present evil age, or are we living in our
spirit? Are we living in religion, or are we walking in spirit? To walk
in spirit means to walk in our spirit. It is in our spirit that we have
the enjoyment of the Lord. This is why this verse says that the Lord's
grace is with our spirit. When we get into our spirit, we enjoy the
Lord as grace. When we begin to quarrel,…we must run back to the
spirit. The more we stay in our mind, the more we will exchange
words. But when we get into our spirit, we touch the grace of the
Lord. Grace is the Lord experienced by us. The experienced Christ
becomes our grace. Here we could never exchange words because
we are in another country. The mind is a quarreling country, but
the spirit is a country of grace. It is not a matter of trying to overcome, it is a matter of being in the right country…[of] our spirit.
(*The Indwelling Christ in the Canons of the New Testament*, p. 111)

Today's Reading

Paul begins the book of Galatians by speaking about Christ.
Then he changes to the Spirit. Eventually, he tells us that the
Spirit, who is the reality of Christ, is in our spirit. Therefore, we
must learn to stay in our spirit. In order to do this we need some
exercise. By our natural birth and life, we live not in our spirit, but
in our mind. But now we must change countries. We must learn
continually to return to the country of grace which is our spirit.

Very few Christians today know that Christ is in their spirit. Hardly anyone has ever paid any attention to the last verse of Galatians....Satan is so subtle. Whenever anyone comes to this verse, he covers these three words: *with your spirit*. The satanic hand hid these three words from me for many years....But the whole book of Galatians is contained in these three words. We can have all the electrical wires installed into a building, yet if we don't have a switch, we cannot apply the electricity. This is the satanic deceit. These three words are the switch. Without them, how and where shall we touch Christ? Oh, how evil Satan is! He has hidden the switch from God's children. But today we know where the switch is. Hallelujah! Christ is the very God in process, and eventually the processed God is Christ as the life-giving Spirit in our spirit. In our spirit we enjoy the indwelling Christ as our grace. The grace of the Lord Jesus Christ is *with our spirit!*

Grace is simply Christ Himself as our enjoyment. When we come back to our spirit, there is just the sweet enjoyment of Christ. Christ is the life-giving Spirit indwelling our spirit. When we turn to our spirit, we simply enjoy Him as our grace. When we are living in our mind, we are living in a backward country. We should not stay there, but turn to the wonderful country of our spirit. This country is...full of grace. Here we have Christ as our full enjoyment.

The book of Galatians starts negatively with the evil age of religion, and it closes positively with the human spirit....We have been delivered out of religion, which was mostly in our mind, to the wonderful enjoyment of Christ in our spirit. Religion has the doctrines, the regulations, the traditions, and the ordinances. But in our spirit we have the living Spirit as the reality of Christ. This is why, when a person stays in his spirit enjoying Christ as grace, he is in another country. He was in the mind, but now he is in his spirit. He was in religion, but now he is enjoying Christ as his grace. (*The Indwelling Christ in the Canons of the New Testament,* pp. 111-113)

Further Reading: The Indwelling Christ in the Canons of the New Testament, ch. 12; *The Living and Practical Way to Enjoy Christ,* ch. 8

Enlightenment and inspiration: _____

_____

_____

_____

Morning Nourishment

Gal. **The grace of our Lord Jesus Christ be with your**
6:18 **spirit, brothers. Amen.**
Heb. **...Who has trampled underfoot the Son of God and...**
10:29 **insulted the Spirit of grace?**
4:16 **Let us therefore come forward with boldness to the**
throne of grace that we may receive mercy and find
grace for timely help.

We have emphasized the fact that grace is God becoming our enjoyment, that grace is Christ enjoyed by us. Now we need to lay equal stress on the fact that grace is actually the Spirit. Grace is God the Father embodied in the Son and the Son realized as the Spirit. Therefore, ultimately, the Spirit is the very grace.

From our experience we know that when we enjoy grace, we enjoy the Spirit. Whenever we are short of the experience of the Spirit moving in us and anointing us, we do not have the enjoyment of grace. Grace is the moving, acting, and anointing of the Spirit within us. The more we have the moving of the Spirit, the more grace we enjoy.

This illustration of electrical current helps us to realize that the Spirit of grace is actually the Spirit moving, acting, and anointing within us. This matter is very subjective. When we see grace in this way, we have hit the mark concerning what grace is. Grace, of course, exists as a reality apart from us. But when grace comes into us, in our experience it is the Spirit. The grace which enters into us and becomes our enjoyment is nothing less than the Spirit Himself. (*Life-study of Galatians,* p. 329)

Today's Reading

How then do we receive grace and enjoy it? If we would receive grace and enjoy grace, we need to realize that our spirit is the only place we can experience grace. Just as electricity can be applied only by turning on the switch, so we can contact the moving, anointing Spirit only in our spirit. If you wish to receive grace and enjoy grace, do not exercise your mind, emotion, or will. Instead, turn to your spirit and exercise it. Brothers are usually quite active in the mind, and sisters are usually very strong in the emotion. We need to turn from our mind and emotion back to the spirit, where we shall meet the Lord.

We thank the Lord for revealing to us where He is today. There can be no doubt that, on the one hand, He is on the throne in heaven. But, on the other hand, for our experience He is in our spirit. Hebrews 4:16 says, "Let us therefore come forward with boldness to the throne of grace that we may receive mercy and find grace for timely help." The throne of grace is not only in heaven; it is also in our spirit. If it were not in our spirit as well as in heaven, how could we come forward to it? Some may argue that our spirit is not large enough to contain the throne of grace. Although this may seem logical in terms of size, the fact that we can come forward to the throne of grace indicates that, experientially, it is in our spirit. From my experience I know that when I turn to my spirit and call, "Lord Jesus," I immediately have the sense that the throne of grace is in my spirit.

Whenever we approach the throne of grace by turning to our spirit and calling on the name of the Lord, we should enthrone the Lord. We must give Him the headship, kingship, and lordship in us. What a tremendous difference this makes! Sometimes as we are praying we sense that the Lord is within us, but we are not willing to give Him the throne. Instead of recognizing His kingship, we exalt ourselves above Him and put ourselves on the throne. In a very practical way, we dethrone the Lord. Whenever we fail to enthrone the Lord, the flow of grace stops. At the very time we are praying, we need to allow the Lord to be on the throne within us, honoring Him as the Head, the Lord, and the King. Then grace will flow within us as a river. (*Life-study of Galatians*, pp. 329-330)

Further Reading: Life-study of Galatians, msg. 37; *A General Sketch of the New Testament in the Light of Christ and the Church, Part 2: Romans through Philemon*, ch. 15

Enlightenment and inspiration: _____

_____

_____

_____

Morning Nourishment

Rev. And he showed me a river of water of life, bright as
22:1 crystal, proceeding out of the throne of God and of
the Lamb in the middle of its street.

Col. And He is the Head of the Body, the church; He is
1:18 the beginning, the Firstborn from the dead, that
He Himself might have the first place in all things.

In Revelation 22:1 and 2 we see that the river of water of life
proceeds out of the throne of God and of the Lamb. God's throne is
thus the source of the flowing grace. To dethrone Him, to take the
throne away from Him, is to disregard the source of grace. This
causes the flow of grace to cease. This is not a mere doctrine, but
something very experiential. Many of us can testify that whenever we fail to enthrone the Lord, we do not receive much grace in
our times of prayer.

If we would receive grace and enjoy grace, the first thing we
must do is turn to our spirit and forget our mind, emotion, and
will. Satan, however, raises up one thing after another to keep us
from the spirit.

The best way to practice turning to the spirit and staying in
the spirit is to have fixed times for prayer. Suppose you set aside
ten minutes in the morning to contact the Lord in prayer. During
this time, the only thing you should do is exercise yourself to turn
to the spirit and stay in the spirit. Do not be concerned about all
the things you must do that day. Reject your natural mind, emotion, and will and exercise your spirit to contact the Lord.
(*Life-study of Galatians*, pp. 330-331)

Today's Reading

The reason so many Christians have little experience of the
Lord is that they do not exercise their spirit. Many simply do not
want to be in the spirit. Furthermore, in his subtlety, Satan seeks to
provoke our mind, emotion, and will. Therefore, it is important for
us to learn to remain in the spirit and not be provoked and drawn
out by the enemy. We need to exercise our spirit to keep our mind,
will, and emotion in their proper place. But if we allow our mind to

be stirred up and our emotion to be provoked, we shall lose many opportunities to minister life to others from our spirit. Instead of using our mind in a natural way and instead of allowing our emotion to be provoked, we should exercise our spirit and pray, "Lord, what do You want me to do, and what do You want me to say? Lord, flow out from my spirit through my words to supply life to those in need." How much better this is than using our natural mind and emotion to deal with situations! What a vast difference this makes! Again and again, I wish to emphasize the fact that our need is to learn to remain in our spirit and to use our spirit.

When we turn to the spirit and stay there, we need to recognize the Lord as the Head and the King and enthrone Him. We need to respect His position, honor His authority, and confess that we have no right to say or do anything on our own. All the ground within us must be given over to the King. If we enthrone the Lord within us, the river of water of life will flow out from the throne to supply us. In this way we shall receive grace and enjoy grace.

Grace is nothing less than the Triune God becoming our enjoyment. The Father is embodied in the Son, and the Son is realized as the Spirit. This Spirit, the ultimate consummation of the Triune God, now dwells in our spirit. Our need today is to turn to this spirit and remain there, enthroning the Lord. Then in a very practical way our spirit will be joined to the third heaven. We shall realize in our experience that, on the one hand, the Holy of Holies is in heaven and that, on the other hand, it is also in our spirit. This indicates that when we remain in our spirit, we actually touch the heavens. If we enthrone the Lord Jesus within us, the Spirit as the water of life will flow from the throne to supply us. This is grace, and this is the way to receive grace and enjoy grace.

As we receive the Triune God as our grace and enjoy Him as grace, we shall be constituted of Him. Little by little, we shall become one with Him organically. He will become our constituent, and we shall become His expression. (*Life-study of Galatians,* pp. 331-332)

Further Reading: Life-study of Galatians, msg. 37

__Enlightenment and inspiration:__ _____

_____

_____

_____

Morning Nourishment

Gal. Henceforth let no one trouble me, for I bear in my
6:17 body the brands of Jesus.

Rom. Paul, a slave of Christ Jesus, a called apostle, sepa-
1:1 rated unto the gospel of God.

John Truly, truly, I say to you, Unless the grain of wheat
12:24 falls into the ground and dies, it abides alone; but if
it dies, it bears much fruit.

The word *brands* in Galatians 6:17 refers to the marks branded on slaves to indicate their owners. With Paul, a slave of Christ (Rom. 1:1), physically the brands were the scars of his wounds received in his faithful service to his Master (2 Cor. 11:23-27). Spiritually, they signify the characteristics of the life he lived, a life like that lived by the Lord Jesus when He was on this earth. Such a life is continually crucified (John 12:24), doing the will of God (John 6:38), seeking not its own glory but the glory of God (John 7:18), and submissive and obedient to God, even unto the death of the cross (Phil. 2:8). Paul followed the pattern of the Lord Jesus, bearing the brands, the characteristics of His life. In this he was absolutely different from the Judaizers. (*Life-study of Galatians*, pp. 272-273)

Today's Reading

Paul considered himself a slave of Christ. Just as a slave might bear a brand mark testifying that he belonged to a certain owner, Paul bore in his body the brands of Jesus. It was as if the name of Christ had been branded upon him again and again as a testimony and declaration that Paul belonged to the Lord.

Paul had been wounded many times because of his faithfulness in service to Christ. In 2 Corinthians 11:24 and 25 he tells us that five times he received "forty stripes less one," that three times he was beaten with rods, and that once he was stoned. Therefore, there were many scars on his body testifying of his years of service to Christ. These scars may also be considered the brands of Jesus.

As we have already indicated, the spiritual significance of the expression "the brands of Jesus" is that Paul lived a crucified life.

When the Lord Jesus was on earth, He took the lead to live such a crucified life. As we read the four Gospels, we see the portrait of a man constantly living a crucified life. This kind of life is a brand. Thus, when the Lord Jesus was on earth, He bore such a brand. He was persecuted, ridiculed, despised, and rejected. However, He did not say anything to defend Himself. Instead, living a crucified life, He bore a brand to show that He belonged to God the Father. Paul followed the Lord Jesus to live this kind of life. In Philippians 3:10 he refers to "the fellowship of His sufferings." As one who lived in the fellowship of Jesus' sufferings, Paul bore the brands of Jesus as the sign that he lived a crucified life. When Paul was greeting the Galatians with a word of peace, he was reminded of the fact that it was the brands of Jesus that kept him in this peace. Because he was persecuted, despised, ridiculed, rejected, and condemned, he could truly say that he bore the brands of Jesus.

Although we do not presume to classify ourselves with Paul, we can say truly that, at least to some extent, we also are bearing the brands of Jesus, for we are ridiculed, mocked, despised, criticized, and condemned. Many evil things are written about us and spoken concerning us. As long as we continue to take the way of the cross, we shall be opposed in this way. If we are faithful to live a crucified life, opposition will rise up again and again. In Galatians 4:29 Paul said, "But just as at that time he who was born according to flesh persecuted him who was born according to Spirit, so also it is now." This word indicates clearly that those who are according to the flesh will persecute those who are according to the Spirit. Just as the Lord Jesus and Paul were persecuted because they lived a crucified life, the same will happen to us if, by the Lord's mercy and grace, we follow their footsteps to live such a life. When we are despised, rejected, condemned, ridiculed, and mocked, we bear the brands of Jesus. However, because we bear these brands, we enjoy peace, and we are not troubled by any situation or circumstances. (*Life-study of Galatians,* pp. 273-274)

Further Reading: Life-study of Galatians, msg. 31

Enlightenment and inspiration: _____

_____

_____

Hymns, #497

1 Grace in its highest definition is
   God in the Son to be enjoyed by us;
   It is not only something done or giv'n,
   But God Himself, our portion glorious.

2 God is incarnate in the flesh that we
   Him may receive, experience ourself;
   This is the grace which we receive of God,
   Which comes thru Christ and which is Christ
      Himself.

3 Paul the Apostle counted all as dung,
   'Twas only God in Christ he counted grace;
   'Tis by this grace—the Lord experienced—
   That he surpassed the others in the race.

4 It is this grace—Christ as our inward strength—
   Which with His all-sufficiency doth fill;
   It is this grace which in our spirit is,
   There energizing, working out God's will.

5 This grace, which is the living Christ Himself,
   Is what we need and must experience;
   Lord, may we know this grace and by it live,
   Thyself increasingly as grace to sense.

*Composition for prophecy with main point and
sub-points:* _____

_____

_____

_____

_____

_____

_____

_____

_____

_____

_____

_____

_____

_____

_____

_____

_____

_____

_____

_____

_____

_____

_____

_____

_____

_____

_____

_____

_____

_____

_____

_____

Reading Schedule for the Recovery Version of the New Testament with Footnotes

Wk.	Lord's Day	Monday	Tuesday	Wednesday	Thursday	Friday	Saturday
1	☐ Matt 1:1-2	☐ 1:3-7	☐ 1:8-17	☐ 1:18-25	☐ 2:1-23	☐ 3:1-6	☐ 3:7-17
2	☐ 4:1-11	☐ 4:12-25	☐ 5:1-4	☐ 5:5-12	☐ 5:13-20	☐ 5:21-26	☐ 5:27-48
3	☐ 6:1-8	☐ 6:9-18	☐ 6:19-34	☐ 7:1-12	☐ 7:13-29	☐ 8:1-13	☐ 8:14-22
4	☐ 8:23-34	☐ 9:1-13	☐ 9:14-17	☐ 9:18-34	☐ 9:35—10:5	☐ 10:6-25	☐ 10:26-42
5	☐ 11:1-15	☐ 11:16-30	☐ 12:1-14	☐ 12:15-32	☐ 12:33-42	☐ 12:43—13:2	☐ 13:3-12
6	☐ 13:13-30	☐ 13:31-43	☐ 13:44-58	☐ 14:1-13	☐ 14:14-21	☐ 14:22-36	☐ 15:1-20
7	☐ 15:21-31	☐ 15:32-39	☐ 16:1-12	☐ 16:13-20	☐ 16:21-28	☐ 17:1-13	☐ 17:14-27
8	☐ 18:1-14	☐ 18:15-22	☐ 18:23-35	☐ 19:1-15	☐ 19:16-30	☐ 20:1-16	☐ 20:17-34
9	☐ 21:1-11	☐ 21:12-22	☐ 21:23-32	☐ 21:33-46	☐ 22:1-22	☐ 22:23-33	☐ 22:34-46
10	☐ 23:1-12	☐ 23:13-39	☐ 24:1-14	☐ 24:15-31	☐ 24:32-51	☐ 25:1-13	☐ 25:14-30
11	☐ 25:31-46	☐ 26:1-16	☐ 26:17-35	☐ 26:36-46	☐ 26:47-64	☐ 26:65-75	☐ 27:1-26
12	☐ 27:27-44	☐ 27:45-56	☐ 27:57—28:15	☐ 28:16-20	☐ Mark 1:1	☐ 1:2-6	☐ 1:7-13
13	☐ 1:14-28	☐ 1:29-45	☐ 2:1-12	☐ 2:13-28	☐ 3:1-19	☐ 3:20-35	☐ 4:1-25
14	☐ 4:26-41	☐ 5:1-20	☐ 5:21-43	☐ 6:1-29	☐ 6:30-56	☐ 7:1-23	☐ 7:24-37
15	☐ 8:1-26	☐ 8:27—9:1	☐ 9:2-29	☐ 9:30-50	☐ 10:1-16	☐ 10:17-34	☐ 10:35-52
16	☐ 11:1-16	☐ 11:17-33	☐ 12:1-27	☐ 12:28-44	☐ 13:1-13	☐ 13:14-37	☐ 14:1-26
17	☐ 14:27-52	☐ 14:53-72	☐ 15:1-15	☐ 15:16-47	☐ 16:1-8	☐ 16:9-20	☐ Luke 1:1-4
18	☐ 1:5-25	☐ 1:26-46	☐ 1:47-56	☐ 1:57-80	☐ 2:1-8	☐ 2:9-20	☐ 2:21-39
19	☐ 2:40-52	☐ 3:1-20	☐ 3:21-38	☐ 4:1-13	☐ 4:14-30	☐ 4:31-44	☐ 5:1-26
20	☐ 5:27—6:16	☐ 6:17-38	☐ 6:39-49	☐ 7:1-17	☐ 7:18-23	☐ 7:24-35	☐ 7:36-50
21	☐ 8:1-15	☐ 8:16-25	☐ 8:26-39	☐ 8:40-56	☐ 9:1-17	☐ 9:18-26	☐ 9:27-36
22	☐ 9:37-50	☐ 9:51-62	☐ 10:1-11	☐ 10:12-24	☐ 10:25-37	☐ 10:38-42	☐ 11:1-13
23	☐ 11:14-26	☐ 11:27-36	☐ 11:37-54	☐ 12:1-12	☐ 12:13-21	☐ 12:22-34	☐ 12:35-48
24	☐ 12:49-59	☐ 13:1-9	☐ 13:10-17	☐ 13:18-30	☐ 13:31—14:6	☐ 14:7-14	☐ 14:15-24
25	☐ 14:25-35	☐ 15:1-10	☐ 15:11-21	☐ 15:22-32	☐ 16:1-13	☐ 16:14-22	☐ 16:23-31
26	☐ 17:1-19	☐ 17:20-37	☐ 18:1-14	☐ 18:15-30	☐ 18:31-43	☐ 19:1-10	☐ 19:11-27

Reading Schedule for the Recovery Version of the New Testament with Footnotes

Wk.	Lord's Day	Monday	Tuesday	Wednesday	Thursday	Friday	Saturday
27	☐ Luke 19:28-48	☐ 20:1-19	☐ 20:20-38	☐ 20:39—21:4	☐ 21:5-27	☐ 21:28-38	☐ 22:1-20
28	☐ 22:21-38	☐ 22:39-54	☐ 22:55-71	☐ 23:1-43	☐ 23:44-56	☐ 24:1-12	☐ 24:13-35
29	☐ 24:36-53	☐ John 1:1-13	☐ 1:14-18	☐ 1:19-34	☐ 1:35-51	☐ 2:1-11	☐ 2:12-22
30	☐ 2:23—3:13	☐ 3:14-21	☐ 3:22-36	☐ 4:1-14	☐ 4:15-26	☐ 4:27-42	☐ 4:43-54
31	☐ 5:1-16	☐ 5:17-30	☐ 5:31-47	☐ 6:1-15	☐ 6:16-31	☐ 6:32-51	☐ 6:52-71
32	☐ 7:1-9	☐ 7:10-24	☐ 7:25-36	☐ 7:37-52	☐ 7:53—8:11	☐ 8:12-27	☐ 8:28-44
33	☐ 8:45-59	☐ 9:1-13	☐ 9:14-34	☐ 9:35—10:9	☐ 10:10-30	☐ 10:31—11:4	☐ 11:5-22
34	☐ 11:23-40	☐ 11:41-57	☐ 12:1-11	☐ 12:12-24	☐ 12:25-36	☐ 12:37-50	☐ 13:1-11
35	☐ 13:12-30	☐ 13:31-38	☐ 14:1-6	☐ 14:7-20	☐ 14:21-31	☐ 15:1-11	☐ 15:12-27
36	☐ 16:1-15	☐ 16:16-33	☐ 17:1-5	☐ 17:6-13	☐ 17:14-24	☐ 17:25—18:11	☐ 18:12-27
37	☐ 18:28-40	☐ 19:1-16	☐ 19:17-30	☐ 19:31-42	☐ 20:1-13	☐ 20:14-18	☐ 20:19-22
38	☐ 20:23-31	☐ 21:1-14	☐ 21:15-22	☐ 21:23-25	☐ Acts 1:1-8	☐ 1:9-14	☐ 1:15-26
39	☐ 2:1-13	☐ 2:14-21	☐ 2:22-36	☐ 2:37-41	☐ 2:42-47	☐ 3:1-18	☐ 3:19—4:22
40	☐ 4:23-37	☐ 5:1-16	☐ 5:17-32	☐ 5:33-42	☐ 6:1—7:1	☐ 7:2-29	☐ 7:30-60
41	☐ 8:1-13	☐ 8:14-25	☐ 8:26-40	☐ 9:1-19	☐ 9:20-43	☐ 10:1-16	☐ 10:17-33
42	☐ 10:34-48	☐ 11:1-18	☐ 11:19-30	☐ 12:1-25	☐ 13:1-12	☐ 13:13-43	☐ 13:44—14:5
43	☐ 14:6-28	☐ 15:1-12	☐ 15:13-34	☐ 15:35—16:5	☐ 16:6-18	☐ 16:19-40	☐ 17:1-18
44	☐ 17:19-34	☐ 18:1-17	☐ 18:18-28	☐ 19:1-20	☐ 19:21-41	☐ 20:1-12	☐ 20:13-38
45	☐ 21:1-14	☐ 21:15-26	☐ 21:27-40	☐ 22:1-21	☐ 22:22-29	☐ 22:30—23:11	☐ 23:12-15
46	☐ 23:16-30	☐ 23:31—24:21	☐ 24:22—25:5	☐ 25:6-27	☐ 26:1-13	☐ 26:14-32	☐ 27:1-26
47	☐ 27:27—28:10	☐ 28:11-22	☐ 28:23-31	☐ Rom 1:1-2	☐ 1:3-7	☐ 1:8-17	☐ 1:18-25
48	☐ 1:26—2:10	☐ 2:11-29	☐ 3:1-20	☐ 3:21-31	☐ 4:1-12	☐ 4:13-25	☐ 5:1-11
49	☐ 5:12-17	☐ 5:18—6:5	☐ 6:6-11	☐ 6:12-23	☐ 7:1-12	☐ 7:13-25	☐ 8:1-2
50	☐ 8:3-6	☐ 8:7-13	☐ 8:14-25	☐ 8:26-39	☐ 9:1-18	☐ 9:19—10:3	☐ 10:4-15
51	☐ 10:16—11:10	☐ 11:11-22	☐ 11:23-36	☐ 12:1-3	☐ 12:4-21	☐ 13:1-14	☐ 14:1-12
52	☐ 14:13-23	☐ 15:1-13	☐ 15:14-33	☐ 16:1-5	☐ 16:6-24	☐ 16:25-27	☐ I Cor 1:1-4

Reading Schedule for the Recovery Version of the New Testament with Footnotes

Wk.	Lord's Day	Monday	Tuesday	Wednesday	Thursday	Friday	Saturday
53	☐ I Cor 1:5-9	☐ 1:10-17	☐ 1:18-31	☐ 2:1-5	☐ 2:6-10	☐ 2:11-16	☐ 3:1-9
54	☐ 3:10-13	☐ 3:14-23	☐ 4:1-9	☐ 4:10-21	☐ 5:1-13	☐ 6:1-11	☐ 6:12-20
55	☐ 7:1-16	☐ 7:17-24	☐ 7:25-40	☐ 8:1-13	☐ 9:1-15	☐ 9:16-27	☐ 10:1-4
56	☐ 10:5-13	☐ 10:14-33	☐ 11:1-6	☐ 11:7-16	☐ 11:17-26	☐ 11:27-34	☐ 12:1-11
57	☐ 12:12-22	☐ 12:23-31	☐ 13:1-13	☐ 14:1-12	☐ 14:13-25	☐ 14:26-33	☐ 14:34-40
58	☐ 15:1-19	☐ 15:20-28	☐ 15:29-34	☐ 15:35-49	☐ 15:50-58	☐ 16:1-9	☐ 16:10-24
59	☐ II Cor 1:1-4	☐ 1:5-14	☐ 1:15-22	☐ 1:23—2:11	☐ 2:12-17	☐ 3:1-6	☐ 3:7-11
60	☐ 3:12-18	☐ 4:1-6	☐ 4:7-12	☐ 4:13-18	☐ 5:1-8	☐ 5:9-15	☐ 5:16-21
61	☐ 6:1-13	☐ 6:14—7:4	☐ 7:5-16	☐ 8:1-15	☐ 8:16-24	☐ 9:1-15	☐ 10:1-6
62	☐ 10:7-18	☐ 11:1-15	☐ 11:16-33	☐ 12:1-10	☐ 12:11-21	☐ 13:1-10	☐ 13:11-14
63	☐ Gal 1:1-5	☐ 1:6-14	☐ 1:15-24	☐ 2:1-13	☐ 2:14-21	☐ 3:1-4	☐ 3:5-14
64	☐ 3:15-22	☐ 3:23-29	☐ 4:1-7	☐ 4:8-20	☐ 4:21-31	☐ 5:1-12	☐ 5:13-21
65	☐ 5:22-26	☐ 6:1-10	☐ 6:11-15	☐ 6:16-18	☐ Eph 1:1-3	☐ 1:4-6	☐ 1:7-10
66	☐ 1:11-14	☐ 1:15-18	☐ 1:19-23	☐ 2:1-5	☐ 2:6-10	☐ 2:11-14	☐ 2:15-18
67	☐ 2:19-22	☐ 3:1-7	☐ 3:8-13	☐ 3:14-18	☐ 3:19-21	☐ 4:1-4	☐ 4:5-10
68	☐ 4:11-16	☐ 4:17-24	☐ 4:25-32	☐ 5:1-10	☐ 5:11-21	☐ 5:22-26	☐ 5:27-33
69	☐ 6:1-9	☐ 6:10-14	☐ 6:15-18	☐ 6:19-24	☐ Phil 1:1-7	☐ 1:8-18	☐ 1:19-26
70	☐ 1:27—2:4	☐ 2:5-11	☐ 2:12-16	☐ 2:17-30	☐ 3:1-6`	☐ 3:7-11	☐ 3:12-16
71	☐ 3:17-21	☐ 4:1-9	☐ 4:10-23	☐ Col 1:1-8	☐ 1:9-13	☐ 1:14-23	☐ 1:24-29
72	☐ 2:1-7	☐ 2:8-15	☐ 2:16-23	☐ 3:1-4	☐ 3:5-15	☐ 3:16-25	☐ 4:1-18
73	☐ I Thes 1:1-3	☐ 1:4-10	☐ 2:1-12	☐ 2:13—3:5	☐ 3:6-13	☐ 4:1-10	☐ 4:11—5:11
74	☐ 5:12-28	☐ II Thes 1:1-12	☐ 2:1-17	☐ 3:1-18	☐ I Tim 1:1-2	☐ 1:3-4	☐ 1:5-14
75	☐ 1:15-20	☐ 2:1-7	☐ 2:8-15	☐ 3:1-13	☐ 3:14—4:5	☐ 4:6-16	☐ 5:1-25
76	☐ 6:1-10	☐ 6:11-21	☐ II Tim 1:1-10	☐ 1:11-18	☐ 2:1-15	☐ 2:16-26	☐ 3:1-13
77	☐ 3:14—4:8	☐ 4:9-22	☐ Titus 1:1-4	☐ 1:5-16	☐ 2:1-15	☐ 3:1-8	☐ 3:9-15
78	☐ Philem 1:1-11	☐ 1:12-25	☐ Heb 1:1-2	☐ 1:3-5	☐ 1:6-14	☐ 2:1-9	☐ 2:10-18

Reading Schedule for the Recovery Version of the New Testament with Footnotes

Wk.	Lord's Day	Monday	Tuesday	Wednesday	Thursday	Friday	Saturday
79	Heb 3:1-6	3:7-19	4:1-9	4:10-13	4:14-16	5:1-10	5:11—6:3
80	6:4-8	6:9-20	7:1-10	7:11-28	8:1-6	8:7-13	9:1-4
81	9:5-14	9:15-28	10:1-18	10:19-28	10:29-39	11:1-6	11:7-19
82	11:20-31	11:32-40	12:1-2	12:3-13	12:14-17	12:18-26	12:27-29
83	13:1-7	13:8-12	13:13-15	13:16-25	James1:1-8	1:9-18	1:19-27
84	2:1-13	2:14-26	3:1-18	4:1-10	4:11-17	5:1-12	5:13-20
85	I Pet 1:1-2	1:3-4	1:5	1:6-9	1:10-12	1:13-17	1:18-25
86	2:1-3	2:4-8	2:9-17	2:18-25	3:1-13	3:14-22	4:1-6
87	4:7-16	4:17-19	5:1-4	5:5-9	5:10-14	II Pet 1:1-2	1:3-4
88	1:5-8	1:9-11	1:12-18	1:19-21	2:1-3	2:4-11	2:12-22
89	3:1-6	3:7-9	3:10-12	3:13-15	3:16	3:17-18	I John 1:1-2
90	1:3-4	1:5	1:6	1:7	1:8-10	2:1-2	2:3-11
91	2:12-14	2:15-19	2:20-23	2:24-27	2:28-29	3:1-5	3:6-10
92	3:11-18	3:19-24	4:1-6	4:7-11	4:12-15	4:16—5:3	5:4-13
93	5:14-17	5:18-21	II John 1:1-3	1:4-9	1:10-13	III John 1:1-6	1:7-14
94	Jude 1:1-4	1:5-10	1:11-19	1:20-25	Rev 1:1-3	1:4-6	1:7-11
95	1:12-13	1:14-16	1:17-20	2:1-6	2:7	2:8-9	2:10-11
96	2:12-14	2:15-17	2:18-23	2:24-29	3:1-3	3:4-6	3:7-9
97	3:10-13	3:14-18	3:19-22	4:1-5	4:6-7	4:8-11	5:1-6
98	5:7-14	6:1-8	6:9-17	7:1-8	7:9-17	8:1-6	8:7-12
99	8:13—9:11	9:12-21	10:1-4	10:5-11	11:1-4	11:5-14	11:15-19
100	12:1-4	12:5-9	12:10-18	13:1-10	13:11-18	14:1-5	14:6-12
101	14:13-20	15:1-8	16:1-12	16:13-21	17:1-6	17:7-18	18:1-8
102	18:9—19:4	19:5-10	19:11-16	19:17-21	20:1-6	20:7-10	20:11-15
103	21:1	21:2	21:3-8	21:9-13	21:14-18	21:19-21	21:22-27
104	22:1	22:2	22:3-11	22:12-15	22:16-17	22:18-21	

Week 1 — Day 1 — Today's verses

Eph. 3:17 That Christ may make His home in your hearts through faith...

Gal. 4:19 My children, with whom I travail again in birth until Christ is formed in you.

3:26 For you are all sons of God through faith in Christ Jesus.

Gal. 2:20 I am crucified with Christ; and it is no longer I who live, but it is Christ who lives in me...

3:3 Are you so foolish? Having begun by the Spirit, are you now being perfected by the flesh?

6:14 But far be it from me to boast except in the cross of our Lord Jesus Christ, through whom the world has been crucified to me and I to the world.

Phil. 1:21 For to me, to live is Christ...

Date

Week 1 — Day 2 — Today's verses

Gal. 3:24 So then the law has become our child-conductor unto Christ that we might be justified out of faith.

1:14-16 And I advanced in Judaism beyond many contemporaries in my race, being more abundantly a zealot for the traditions of my fathers. But when it pleased God...to reveal His Son in me...

Gal. 1:1 Paul, an apostle (not from men nor through man but through Jesus Christ and God the Father, who raised Him from the dead).

6:15 For neither is circumcision anything nor uncircumcision, but a new creation *is what matters.*

Eph. 4:24 And put on the new man, which was created according to God in righteousness and holiness of the reality.

Date

Week 1 — Day 3 — Today's verses

Gal. 4:4-7 But when the fullness of the time came, God sent forth His Son, born of a woman, born under law, that He might redeem those under law that we might receive the sonship. And because you are sons, God has sent forth the Spirit of His Son into our hearts, crying, Abba, Father! So then you are no longer a slave but a son; and if a son, an heir also through God.

Gal. 6:15 For neither is circumcision anything nor uncircumcision, but a new creation is what matters.

1 John 4:15 Whoever confesses that Jesus is the Son of God, God abides in him and he in God.

2 Cor. 5:17 So then if anyone is in Christ, he is a new creation. The old things have passed away; behold, they have become new.

Date

Gal.
1:13-16 For you have heard of my manner of life formerly in Judaism, that I persecuted the church of God excessively and ravaged it. And I advanced in Judaism beyond many contemporaries in my race, being more abundantly a zealot for the traditions of my fathers. But when it pleased God, who set me apart from my mother's womb and called me through His grace, to reveal His Son in me that I might announce Him as the gospel among the Gentiles...

_____
Date

Gal.
1:15-16 But when it pleased God...to reveal His Son in me,...immediately I did not confer with flesh and blood.

2:20 I am crucified with Christ; and it is no longer I who live, but it is Christ who lives in me...

4:19 My children, with whom I travail again in birth until Christ is formed in you.

Eph.
1:17 That the God of our Lord Jesus Christ, the Father of glory, may give to you a spirit of wisdom and revelation in the full knowledge of Him.

2 Cor.
3:15-16 Indeed unto this day, whenever Moses is read, a veil lies on their heart; but whenever their heart turns to the Lord, the veil is taken away.

4:3-4 And even if our gospel is veiled, it is veiled in those who are perishing, in whom the god of this age has blinded the thoughts of the unbelievers that the illumination of the gospel of the glory of Christ, who is the image of God, might not shine on them.

_____
Date

Week 2 — Day 1   Today's verses

Gal.
1:4 Who gave Himself for our sins that He might rescue us out of the present evil age according to the will of our God and Father.

John
10:3 To him the doorkeeper opens, and the sheep hear his voice; and he calls his own sheep by name and leads them out.

16 And I have other sheep, which are not of this fold; I must lead them also, and they shall hear My voice, and there shall be one flock, one Shepherd.

_____
Date

Week 2 — Day 2   Today's verses

S. S.
1:6-8 ...My mother's sons were angry with me; they made me keeper of the vineyards, but my own vineyard I have not kept. Tell me, you whom my soul loves, where do you pasture your flock? Where do you make it lie down at noon? For why should I be like one who is veiled beside the flocks of your companions? If you yourself do not know, you fairest among women, go forth on the footsteps of the flock...

John
10:16 And I have other sheep, which are not of this fold; I must lead them also, and they shall hear My voice, and there shall be one flock, one Shepherd.

_____
Date

Week 2 — Day 3   Today's verses

John
4:24 God is Spirit, and those who worship Him must worship in spirit and truthfulness.

Eph.
2:22 In whom you also are being built together into a dwelling place of God in spirit.

Rom.
8:2 For the law of the Spirit of life has freed me in Christ Jesus from the law of sin and of death.

1 Pet.
2:9 But you are a chosen race, a royal priesthood, a holy nation...

_____
Date

Week 3 — Day 1

Today's verses

Eph. 1:5 Predestinating us unto sonship through Jesus Christ to Himself, according to the good pleasure of His will.

Gal. 1:4 Who gave Himself for our sins that He might rescue us out of the present evil age according to the will of our God and Father.

4:19 My children, with whom I travail again in birth until Christ is formed in you.

Gal. 2:20 I am crucified with Christ; and it is no longer I who live, but it is Christ who lives in me; and the life which I now live in the flesh I live in faith, the faith of the Son of God, who loved me and gave Himself up for me.

3:14 In order that the blessing of Abraham might come to the Gentiles in Christ Jesus, that we might receive the promise of the Spirit through faith.

Rom. 6:4 We have been buried therefore with Him through baptism into His death, in order that just as Christ was raised from the dead through the glory of the Father, so also we might walk in newness of life.

Date _____

Week 3 — Day 2

Today's verses

Gen. 3:15 And I will put enmity between you and the woman and between your seed and her seed; he will bruise you on the head, but you will bruise him on the heel.

Gal. 3:16 But to Abraham were the promises spoken and to his seed. He does not say, "And to the seeds," as concerning many, but as concerning one: "And to your seed," who is Christ.

4:4 But when the fullness of the time came, God sent forth His Son, born of a woman, born under law.

Gal. 4:19 My children, with whom I travail again in birth until Christ is formed in you.

5:16 But I say, Walk by the Spirit and you shall by no means fulfill the lust of the flesh.

25 If we live by the Spirit, let us also walk by the Spirit.

Rom. 12:2 And do not be fashioned according to this age, but be transformed by the renewing of the mind...

Date _____

Week 3 — Day 3

Today's verses

Gal. 3:2 This only I wish to learn from you, Did you receive the Spirit out of the works of law or out of the hearing of faith?

Rom. 10:17 So faith comes out of hearing, and hearing through the word of Christ.

Heb. 11:6 But without faith it is impossible to be well pleasing to Him, for he who comes forward to God must believe that He is and that He is a rewarder of those who diligently seek Him.

Gal. 6:8 ...He who sows unto the Spirit will of the Spirit reap eternal life.

14-15 But far be it from me to boast except in the cross of our Lord Jesus Christ, through whom the world has been crucified to me and I to the world. For neither is circumcision anything nor uncircumcision, but a new creation is what matters.

18 The grace of our Lord Jesus Christ be with your spirit, brothers. Amen.

Date _____

Gen. And I will put enmity between you and
3:15 the woman and between your seed and her seed; he will bruise you on the head, but you will bruise him on the heel.

Heb. Since therefore the children have shared
2:14 in blood and flesh, He also Himself in like manner partook of the same, that through death He might destroy him who has the might of death, that is, the devil.

Gal. In order that the blessing of Abraham
3:14 might come to the Gentiles in Christ Jesus, that we might receive the promise of the Spirit through faith.

Date

Gal. And that by law no one is justified before
3:11 God is evident because, "The righteous one shall have life and live by faith."

2:19-20 For I through law have died to law that I might live to God. I am crucified with Christ; and it is no longer I who live, but it is Christ who lives in me; and the life which I now live in the flesh I live in faith, the faith of the Son of God, who loved me and gave Himself up for me.

Date

Matt. And Peter answered and said to Jesus,
17:4-5 Lord, it is good for us to be here; if You are willing, I will make three tents here, one for You and one for Moses and one for Elijah. While he was still speaking, behold, a bright cloud overshadowed them, and behold, a voice out of the cloud, saying, This is My Son, the Beloved, in whom I have found My delight. Hear Him!

8 And when they lifted up their eyes, they saw no one except Jesus Himself alone.

Rom. For Christ is the end of the law unto righ-
10:4 teousness to everyone who believes.

Date

Col. Of which I became a minister according
1:25 to the stewardship of God, which was given to me for you, to complete the word of God.

Rom. Paul, a slave of Christ Jesus, a called apos-
1:1 tle, separated unto the gospel of God.

9 For God is my witness, whom I serve in my spirit in the gospel of His Son, how unceasingly I make mention of you always in my prayers.

12:5 So we who are many are one Body in Christ, and individually members one of another.

Date

Gal. 2:5 To them we yielded with the subjection demanded not even for an hour, that the truth of the gospel might remain with you.

16 And knowing that a man is not justified out of works of law, but through faith in Jesus Christ, we also have believed into Christ Jesus that we might be justified out of faith in Christ and not out of the works of law, because out of the works of law no flesh will be justified.

5:6 For in Christ Jesus neither circumcision avails anything nor uncircumcision, but faith avails, operating through love.

Date

Gal. To reveal His Son in me that I might an-
1:16 nounce Him as the gospel among the Gentiles, immediately I did not confer with flesh and blood.

3:26-27 For you are all sons of God through faith in Christ Jesus. For as many of you as were baptized into Christ have put on Christ.

4:19 My children, with whom I travail again in birth until Christ is formed in you.

Date

Gal. I am crucified with Christ; and it is no
2:20 longer I who live, but it is Christ who
lives in me; and the life which I now live
in the flesh I live in faith, the faith of the
Son of God, who loved me and gave
Himself up for me.

4:19 My children, with whom I travail again in
birth until Christ is formed in you.

Date

Gal. For I through law have died to law that I
2:19-20 might live to God. I am crucified with
Christ; and it is no longer I who live, but it
is Christ who lives in me; and the life
which I now live in the flesh I live in faith,
the faith of the Son of God, who loved me
and gave Himself up for me.

Date

John As the living Father has sent Me and I live
6:57 because of the Father, so he who eats Me,
he also shall live because of Me.

14:19 Yet a little while and the world beholds
Me no longer, but you behold Me; because I live, you also shall live.

Phil. As to zeal, persecuting the church; as to
3:6 the righteousness which is in the law, become blameless.

Date

Week 5 — Day 1   Today's verses

Gal. For I through law have died to law that I
2:19 might live to God.

Rom. For if we have grown together with *Him* in
6:5 the likeness of His death, indeed we will
also be *in the likeness* of His resurrection.

7:4 So then, my brothers, you also have been
made dead to the law through the body of
Christ so that you might be joined to another, to Him who has been raised from the
dead, that we might bear fruit to God.

11:16-17 ...And if the root is holy, the branches are
also. But... you, being a wild olive tree,
were grafted in among them and became a
fellow partaker of the root of fatness of the
olive tree.

Date

Week 5 — Day 2   Today's verses

John Abide in Me and I in you. As the branch
15:4 cannot bear fruit of itself unless it abides
in the vine, so neither can you unless you
abide in Me.

14:20 In that day you will know that I am in My
Father, and you in Me, and I in you.

1 Cor. But he who is joined to the Lord is one
6:17 spirit.

Date

Week 5 — Day 3   Today's verses

Gal. For I through law have died to law that I
2:19 might live to God.

6:14 But far be it from me to boast except in
the cross of our Lord Jesus Christ, through
whom the world has been crucified to me
and I to the world.

Rom. We have been buried therefore with Him
6:4 through baptism into His death, in order
that just as Christ was raised from the
dead through the glory of the Father, so
also we might walk in newness of life.

Date

Gal. The grace of our Lord Jesus Christ be with
6:18 your spirit, brothers. Amen.
Heb. ...Who has trampled underfoot the Son
10:29 of God and... insulted the Spirit of grace?
Gal. Let us therefore come forward with bold-
4:16 ness to the throne of grace that we may
receive mercy and find grace for timely
help.

_____
Date

Week 6 — Day 1   **Today's verses**

Gal. I am crucified with Christ; and it is no
2:20-21 longer I who live, but it is Christ who
lives in me; and the life which I now live
in the flesh I live in faith, the faith of the
Son of God, who loved me and gave
Himself up for me. I do not nullify the
grace of God; for if righteousness is
through law, then Christ has died for
nothing.
5:25 If we live by the Spirit, let us also walk by
the Spirit.

_____
Date

Rev. And he showed me a river of water of life,
22:1 bright as crystal, proceeding out of the
throne of God and of the Lamb in the
middle of its street.
Col. And He is the Head of the Body, the
1:18 church; He is the beginning, the Firstborn
from the dead, that He Himself might
have the first place in all things.

_____
Date

Week 6 — Day 2   **Today's verses**

Gal. You have been brought to nought, sepa-
5:4 rated from Christ, you who are being justified by law; you have fallen from grace.
John Abide in Me and I in you. As the branch
15:4-5 cannot bear fruit of itself unless it abides
in the vine, so neither can you unless you
abide in Me. I am the vine; you are the
branches. He who abides in Me and I in
him, he bears much fruit; for apart from
Me you can do nothing.

_____
Date

Gal. Henceforth let no one trouble me, for I
6:17 bear in my body the brands of Jesus.
Rom. Paul, a slave of Christ Jesus, a called apos-
1:1 tle, separated unto the gospel of God.
John Truly, truly, I say to you, Unless the grain
12:24 of wheat falls into the ground and dies, it
abides alone; but if it dies, it bears much
fruit.

_____
Date

Week 6 — Day 3   **Today's verses**

Gal. Who gave Himself for our sins that He
1:4 might rescue us out of the present evil age
according to the will of our God and Father.
6:18 The grace of our Lord Jesus Christ be with
your spirit, brothers. Amen.
John God is Spirit, and those who worship
4:24 Him must worship in spirit and truthfulness.

_____
Date